# THE INDEPENDENT

# NEW YORK CITY 2017

HANNAH BORENSTEIN (AUTHOR)

AND

GIOVANNI COSTA (EDITOR)

# Contents

# New York City: A Brief History

*In order to understand how New York City has become the 24-hour city it is today, let's look back through time and see how the 'Big Apple' has changed.*

## European Settlement

In the Algonquian language known as Unami, "Lenape" means, "genuine, pure, and original." Also, it was the name of a Native American tribe that ruled the territory along the Delaware River, including parts of modern day Delaware, New Jersey, Pennsylvania, and the area that is now New York City.

Settlers first came to the island of Manhattan in 1609. That year, Englishman Henry Hudson sailed a Dutch East India Company ship, the Half Moon, to the tip of the island. Within a decade, the Dutch West Indian Company was sending African slaves to construct the settlements, including protection from the Native American inhabitants. In 1647, the Dutch were granted power over what they then called "New Amsterdam".

There was a great deal of development including building a protective wall (now Wall Street), a canal into the island (now Broad Street) and the foundations of Broadway. However, by 1667, the English took over the land and renamed it "New York" after the Duke of York.

For the century that followed leading up to the Revolutionary War, African slaves were a significant part of the population. Today, in Lower Manhattan the African Burial Ground Monument holds remains of hundreds of enslaved Africans.

## Post American Revolution

As the Continental Army fought against British troops following the Declaration of Independence, New York was witness to its fair share of bloodshed. It was not until 1783 that the British forces ultimately left the city and shortly after, New York was considered the capital of the United States.

As the 1840s rolled around, NYC began establishing itself as an immigrant city. First the Great Irish Famine brought large numbers of Irish immigrants to New York, and then the Civil War victory and the emancipation of slaves gave New York the image of immigrant opportunities. The Statue of Liberty was given as a gift by French sculptor Frederic Augeste Bartholdi, which was to be a representation of freedom and liberty to those moving to the United States of America.

At the turn of the 20th century, NYC started experiencing rapid and modernizing industrialization.

Pennsylvania Station followed Grand Central Terminal's successful opening, as did the Interborough Rapid Transit (NYC's first subway company).

Additionally, some of the most iconic skyscrapers began to prop up, including the Flatiron Building in 1902 and the Woolworth Building in 1913 (the tallest building in the world until 1930).

Throughout the 1920s and 1940s NYC changed, grew, and flourished. United States minority migrants, as well as international immigrants, fled to New York in droves. This led to NYC becoming a hub for manufacturing and industrialization. Immigrants brought with them their learned trades and created garments, jewelry, and various other products when they arrived to support themselves.

Despite the Great Depression, the city continued to build – the Chrysler building and the Empire State Building were constructed in 1931 and various other significant buildings followed.

# Post World War II

The demographics and numbers of people changed greatly during World War II, and the years following the war were met with uncertainty and alterations. NYC, though seen as a leading city worldwide, was transitioning from its industrial history toward the financial, commercial, and corporate sectors.

The civil rights movements, gang wars, and bohemian movement, brought crime, drugs, and poverty to NYC during the 1970s and 1980s. In 1975, the island found itself close to bankruptcy and the majority of neighborhoods were deemed unsafe to walk through. As the city slowly got back on its feet with effects from the 'dot com' boom and government-funded restoration projects, it began to transform into the identity it maintains today – safer, yet still colored with diversity.

# The City Today

New York City continues to experience substantial changes. The attacks of September 11, 2001 caused devastation to both the physical city, and the morale of its citizens, as did the more recent Hurricane Sandy in 2012. However, the city has continued to preserve its iconic appeal.

Today, New York City is the most populated city in the United States. As of 2014, there were just fewer than 8.5 million residents. With the small geographic space of NYC, this means that the average density is just fewer than 28,000 people per square mile.

In the next few chapters, we cover the essential information you need to visit New York City today,

# NYC: Know Before You Go

*Before we start uncovering the delights of NYC today, here we take a brief look at a selection of information you should know before you arrive.*

## Entering the USA

If you are not a resident of the United States of America, you will need to gain legal entry into the country before planning your trip. There are two ways you can do this:

a) Enter under the Visa Waiver Program
b) Get a Visa

**The Visa Waiver Program:**
The Visa Waiver Program allows eligible travelers to enter the United States without getting a Visa. They will instead need an ESTA (Electronic System for Travel Authorization) which is easier to obtain and much less costly.

The following text comes directly from the Department for Homeland Security:

Who is eligible to apply for admission under the Visa Waiver Program?

You are eligible to apply for admission under the Visa Waiver Program (VWP) if you:

• Intend to enter the United States for 90 days or less for business, pleasure or transit
• Have a valid passport lawfully issued to you by a Visa Waiver Program country (The passport must have be an e-passport)
• Have authorization to travel via the Electronic System for Travel Authorization
• Arrive via a Visa Waiver Program signatory carrier (This includes all major carriers)
• Have a return or onward ticket
• Travel may not terminate in contiguous territory or adjacent islands unless the traveler is a resident of one of those areas
• Are a citizen or national of one of the following Visa Waiver Program countries: Andorra, Australia, Austria, Belgium Brunei, Chile, Czech Republic, Denmark, Estonia, Finland, France, Germany, Greece, Hungary, Iceland, Ireland, Italy, Japan, Latvia, Liechtenstein, Lithuania, Luxembourg, Malta, Monaco, the Netherlands, New Zealand, Norway, Portugal, Republic of Korea, San Marino, Singapore, Slovakia, Slovenia, Spain, Sweden, Switzerland, Taiwan and the United Kingdom.
• Establish to the satisfaction of the inspecting United States Customs and Border Protection officer that you are entitled to be admitted under the Visa Waiver Program and that you are not inadmissible under the Immigration and Nationality Act.
• Waive any rights to review or appeal of the admissibility determination of the United States Customs and Border Protection officer, or contest, other than on the basis of an application for asylum, any removal action arising from an application for admission under the Visa Waiver Program.
• Reaffirm, through the submission of biometric identifiers (including fingerprints and

photographs) during processing upon arrival in the United States, your waiver of any rights to review or appeal of the admissibility determination of the United States Customs and Border Protection officer, or contest, other than on the basis of an application for asylum, any removal action arising from an application for admission under the Visa Waiver Program.
• Obtain an Authorization Approved determination following a travel authorization application.
• Not pose a threat to the welfare, health, safety, or security of the United States.
• Have complied with all conditions of any previous admission under the Visa Waiver Program.

An ESTA to enter the US can be obtained at https://esta.cbp.dhs.gov/esta/ by filling in a long form and agreeing to some statements. There are other services that will offer to do this for you for an additional fee but you may be risking your personal and financial details for no extra benefit, and be paying more. Go to the official website listed above. The fee for an ESTA is $14 per person. The decision may be made within seconds, or it can take up to 72 hours. Make sure to print out your ESTA reference number as it may be required by your airline. Your ESTA is valid for two years and is connected to your passport so if you lose your passport, or it expires, you will a new ESTA.

**Getting a US visa:**
Getting a non-immigrant visa is a longer, complicated and much more arduous process that requires you to make an appointment and visit a US embassy for an interview. It will involve lots of form filling, phone calls, lots of waiting, travelling, and it is also expensive. Unfortunately for those not eligible for an ESTA under the Visa Waiver Program, it is the only way to visit the United States.

# Internet Access

NYC has good cell coverage for data but this is often very expensive for international visitors, so you are best sticking to Wi-Fi hotspots when you need data.

Most hotels will now include unlimited free Wi-Fi in the cost of your room. When out and about, many restaurants also provide free Wi-Fi access for guests of the eating establishment.

McDonalds's and Starbucks are the most common names as far as widespread Wi-Fi, as they provide free Wi-Fi access around town at their locations. If you happen to walk past an Apple Store, you can use their Wi-Fi too.

Many public libraries also provide free access – including the NY Public Library and the Mid-Manhattan Library.

ATT Wireless and CableVision provide free Wi-Fi in New York City's parks – ATT's is unlimited free access, whereas CableVision's is time limited.

# Currency

The currency in use in New York City, as in all the USA, is the US Dollar (USD). Note that cheque, are no longer accepted in the vast majority of establishments.

As such, a mix of cash and credit is recommended. We recommend using a pre-paid card or using a no-fee debit card from your home country.

For UK users, we recommend FairFx's pre-paid debit card service. There is usually a £9.95 fee for the card but by using our exclusive link you get the card for free: http://bit.ly/debitdlp

Visa, Mastercard and American Express are the most widely accepted brands of credit and debit cards, with Maestro and Diners Club being accepted at select establishments.

In the USA, the Chip and Sign system is used and unlike most countries around the world, it is rare for you to be asked for your PIN. Instead you will sign your receipt.

Payment in restaurants, for example, may seem odd to most international visitors. Once you finish your meal and ask for the check, you will receive a receipt with the total price and an area asking how much you would like to tip. Your card will then be swiped for payment for the total amount – initially only the meal price will be deducted and this id adjusted over the following days to include the price of the tip as well.

# Making Phone Calls:

Make sure your mobile or cell phone works in the US. Modern smartphones will most likely work everywhere but some older phones, and non-smartphones, may be limited to your home country or region. Be sure to check before travelling.

You should be aware of roaming charges when visiting the US. Calls and text messages also often cost significantly more than they do back home. You may also be charged to receive calls and messages too. Data, in particular, can be extremely expensive so be sure to check with your network provider whether they offer any roaming deals or packages.

Once in the US, you will need to dial an international code to make calls. For calls to the US, you should add 001 or +1 before the phone number you are calling. Each area of the US has its own area code, for NYC's Manhattan area this is mainly 212. So, if you are dialling an NYC number from your cell phone, you would call 001212 or +1212, then the rest of the number.

If you need to make calls back to your own country when in the US, depending on how your network provider has set this up, you may need to enter your country's international dialling code, followed by the phone number. For the UK, for example, you would need to add +44 before the phone number. Other network providers may allow you to call your home country without the international code – this varies.

# The Local Population

NYC remains the most densely populated city in the United States, and is often considered the most diverse area.

With about 8.5 million residents, NYC has more locals than Los Angeles and Chicago combined. In 2010, the city's population was approximately 44% white, 25% black, 29% Hispanic, and 13% Asian. This does not add up to 100% as some people identify themselves as being of multiple races.

Since the turn of the 20th century when the term "melting pot" was created to refer to the immigrant neighborhoods of Lower Manhattan, diversity has manifested and maintained itself through cultural, religious, and ethnic enclaves, scattered throughout.

Although some groups have moved due to gentrification, some of the largest populations of Asian Americans and Andean Americans in the United States have found homes throughout the metropolis.

People from all walks of life flood the sidewalks of NYC, but it has become known as a bastion of political and social progression.

Homosexuality, in most areas, is celebrated, the homeless will interact with the wealthy, and protesters are common fixtures in major parks.

# The Layout

To Manhattanites, there are four basic directions: North, South, East, and West. NYC is one of the easiest cities to navigate, at least above 14th street, as its grid-formation holds no tricks. In Manhattan, 'streets' run East to West, and 'avenues' run North to South. Thus, if you get out of a subway on 42nd Street and are trying to get to 40th Street, if you walk up one block and see 43rd Street, you know you need to turn around and walk the other way.

Avenues are spaced much further apart than Streets are, and there are only 11. The 12th Avenue is the West Side Highway along the Hudson River. The dividing line between East and West for most of Manhattan is 5th Avenue. Thus, if you see an address that reads 155 W 42nd Street, it will be number 155 West of 5th Avenue.

If you are walking some distance, it is fairly easy to estimate how long it will take you to walk. One block going north/south will take you about 1 minute to walk at a leisurely pace, one block going east/west will take you about 4 minutes.

As you make your way further downtown, past 1st Street on the East Side and past 14th Street on the West Side, the grid does disappear and the layout becomes more similar to many other world cities. The street layout becomes more confusing, not as straight, and less familiar.

We recommend having a paper map with you, as well as a smartphone. This is because although cell phone reception is fine for most of Manhattan, you will find that the GPS regularly gets "confused" due to the large buildings and your location on your smartphone may not be where you thought it was.

# Weather

NYC has seasons, and strong ones at that. The timing of your visit will greatly impact the clothes you bring, and some of the activities you may wish to do. The coldest month is usually January. The average low is about 27 °F (-3 °C), but there will be regular drops to 10 °F (-12 °C) for days and sometimes weeks at a time. Snowfall varies, but in recent years January and February have yielded significant amounts of snow, often over 50 centimeters (20 inches).

Although Summer temperatures lie at a sensible average 82 °F (28 °C), it can feel warmer as humidity levels are high and industrial systems (such as the subway, restaurants, etc.) constantly emit heat that gets trapped in the city streets.

The Spring and the Fall (Autumn) are often unpredictable and fleeting. Temperatures in NYC usually fall within a range, but it is not uncommon for them to be erratic and extreme. But April, May, September, and October are generally considered the mildest months.

Rainfall is relatively consistent throughout the year, with monthly rainfall averaging between 3 and 4 inches. Each month has 10 to 15 rainy days on average, with Spring being the wettest season. February is the month which experiences the least rain but even this is only a marginal difference.

**Month by Month Temperature Averages:**

Temperatures are averages, in Celsius, followed by Fahrenheit.

| Month | Low (C/F) | High (C/F) | Month | Low (C/F) | High (C/F) |
|-------|-----------|------------|-------|-----------|------------|
| January | -3/27 | 6/43 | July | 20/67 | 29/84 |
| February | -3/27 | 7/44 | August | 20/67 | 28/82 |
| March | 1/35 | 9/48 | September | 16/60 | 24/75 |
| April | 6/42 | 16/61 | October | 10/50 | 18/64 |
| May | 12/54 | 20/68 | November | 5/41 | 12/54 |
| June | 17/62 | 27/80 | December | 4/40 | 12/54 |

# Typical NYC Food

When it comes to food and drink, there is nothing NYC doesn't have. Any desired craving can be satisfied, and often within a five-block radius. While quality does vary, with New Yorkers' fairly high standards and rent being high, the food is, by and large, pretty good.

Some Californians will debate the quality of the Mexican food and you will find critics everywhere you go, but because of the tremendous immigrant population a lot of the food at ethnic restaurants is authentic and delicious.

Most importantly, however, is to try the NYC staples. NYC is famed for its bagels, pizza, hot dogs, cheesecake, and other delights. New Yorkers pride themselves on top quality, and will debate for hours about the best place to get a bagel or a slice of pizza. While you will find examples in the neighborhood guides in this book, here are a best of the classics New York.

**Bagels:**
• Absolute Bagels – 2788 Broadway
• Ess-a-Bagel – 831 3rd Avenue
• Brooklyn Bagel & Coffee Company – 286 8th Avenue

**Pizza Slices:**
• Famous Joe's Pizza – 7 Carmine Street
• Sal and Carmine – 2671 Broadway
• Grimaldi's – 656 6th Avenue & 1 Front Street, Brooklyn

**Cheesecake:**
• Junior's – 386 Flatbush Avenue, Brooklyn
• Eileen's Special Cheesecake – 17 Cleveland Place
•Lady M Confections – 41 E 78th Street

**Hot Dogs:**
• Nathan's Famous – 1310 Surf Avenue, Brooklyn
• Gray's Papaya – 2090 Broadway (other locations)
• Dirty Water Hot Dogs – Sold on street corner pushcarts around NYC

# NYC Customs and Etiquette

New Yorkers are notorious for being rude, quick-tempered, and not very warm or welcoming. While this is not entirely untrue, people do not smile at one another or greet one another all the time.

There are ways to bother New Yorkers; remember, the sidewalks, subways, etc. that you are touring – these are streets, neighborhoods, etc. where people live. They just want to be treated as such.

## Walking

Subways, buses, and bikes, are certainly great for traversing longer distances, however, NYC is certainly a place where a great deal of walking could, and should, be done. New Yorkers tend to walk quickly, whether they are in a rush or not, and they do not like to slow down their cadence. If you are with a big group of people, it is a good idea to not take up the entire sidewalk. Always leave a path for people to get around you.

Also, NYC does have a lot of magnificent buildings, interesting people, stores, and images that you are welcome to look at, feel enamored, and snap some photos. However, stopping abruptly on a sidewalk to do so is fairly taboo. It is wise to take a quick look over your shoulder, and pull over to one end of the sidewalk as you would if you were pulling over a car on a highway.

These may seem like small trivialities, but if you are looking to minimize the number of New Yorkers that you upset, these tips will help.

## Elevator Etiquette

Elevator etiquette is very important to residents of NYC. Thus, at hotels, museums, or places where there are mostly tourists, it does not really apply. However, in office buildings and residential buildings, there are a few minor rules to consider.

Many buildings have more than 10 stories. Thus, if everyone gets into an elevator and presses their individual floors, it can take 4 to 5 minutes for the people who live or work up at the top to get off.

Firstly, if you are a healthy adult capable of walking a few flights of stairs, and there are 10 or more flights, it is customary that you walk at least until the 3rd floor (if you are older or have an injury/health condition this does not apply).

Secondly, as the floor numbers get bigger and bigger, this rule changes. Essentially, if you are within a flight or two of a number that has already been pressed, the expectation is that you will normally get out and take a flight down or up. For example, if you are going to the 22nd floor, and you get on an elevator and number 23 has already been pressed, if you press 22 people may scoff at you. It is easy to get off on the 23rd and take the stairs down. Obviously if you are disabled, on crutches, or elderly, this does not apply.

## Smoking

A state-wide ban has been in force since 2003, restricting where people can and cannot smoke. It is illegal to smoke in all enclosed spaces, with a few exceptions including cigar bars, private homes and tobacco

businesses. It is also not allowed on public transportation, including all buses and subways.

Additionally, smoking is forbidden in parks, beaches, pedestrian plazas (like Times Square), swimming pools, boardwalks, and select other locations.

Since 2014, electronic cigarettes are subject to the same restriction as regular cigarettes. The minimum age to buy tobacco, cigarettes and e-cigarettes in New York City is 21.

### Tipping

Tipping in NYC is essentially, although not legally, mandatory. This may come as a shock to many international visitors, but tipping is what pays the majority of many employees' paychecks. Waiters

and waitresses make incredibly small salaries and rely on tips to get by. Even at high-end restaurants, most of the staff live in the outer boroughs; many people in the hospitality industry in NYC are pursuing other careers and dreams, and are keeping a job only to support themselves.

Anywhere between 15 to 20% of the check before taxes is pretty standard. Most New Yorkers tip on the higher end: at least 18%. Tips of 15% are becoming less commonplace. Often with bigger groups – over five or six people – the tip is included, so be careful and read the check every time. Many credit card machines will propose a minimum tip of 20%, but you are free to change this.

Tipping doesn't just stop and wait staff, however. Bartenders will expect $1 per round, bell hops should be rewarded with $1 per bag (more if they are heavy), tour guides are commonly tipped 10% to 15% of the price of a guided tour, and it is common to tip taxi drivers about 15%. If you ask your hotel's concierge service for help, a tip is expected - $1 to $2 for calling you a cab, and $3 to $5 for a restaurant or show reservation – more if these are particularly hard to secure. Be sure to have quite a few $1 bills on you for tips.

# Getting to NYC

*Before you enjoy exploring the 'Big Apple', you first need to get there. For the majority of visitors from around the world this will mean flying in to one of the airports in New York City. However, this is far from the only option: driving, trains and long-distance buses are just some of the other ways to reach the city.*

## Flying

The airports that most people fly into are: LaGuardia Airport, John F. Kennedy (JFK) International Airport, and Newark Liberty International Airport just over the bridge in New Jersey. LaGuardia is primarily a domestic airport while JFK and Newark serve more international flights.

### LaGuardia Airport

Mainly used for flights within the US, La Guardia Airport is in the process of being rebuilt in phases to modernize it. It is the least busy of the three NYC airports.

A bus, the NYC Airporter, runs every 30 minutes to midtown Manhattan – Port Authority, Grand Central Station, and Penn Station. Tickets are $14 each way and can be purchased online at www.NYCAirporter.com or by phone on (718) 777-5111. Other public transit options are the MTA public buses.

The M60 goes to upper Manhattan through Queens and the Q70 takes you to Midtown Manhattan near a lot of subway stops. The bus fare is $2.75 with a MetroCard or you can purchase a $3.00 single ride ticket. There is no direct subway link to or from the airport.

Taxis are available and you should only use certified Yellow Taxis. There are often black cars, known as gypsy cabs, which are illegal and may charge much higher rates. From LaGuardia to Manhattan the fares will be anywhere between $29-$40 before tax and tolls. The taxis are metered which means the more traffic, the more expensive it will be.

Uber and Lyft are also options (use our exclusive link at http://uber.com/invite/uberindependentguides for $20 in free credit).

Car rentals are also available but few people choose to drive in NYC. It is mainly a hassle and parking is often very expensive and cumbersome.

## NEWARK LIBERTY AIRPORT

Newark is the second biggest airport serving New York City and handles both domestic and international flights.

From Newark, there are several transportation options to reach the city.

The Air Train connects to NJ Transit or Amtrak (NJ Transit is cheaper), which will take you to Manhattan's Penn Station. This is the cheaper, and often quickest option. It will cost you $12.50.

There are also a number of private shuttle bus offerings from Newark to Manhattan that range from $15 to $60 each way. Companies include Go Airlink NYC, Newark Liberty Airport Express, Super Shuttle and NYC Airporter.

A taxi from Newark to Manhattan will run you somewhere between $50 to $70, not including tolls. This is a metered fare, and at peak times you are likely to hit a lot of traffic.

## J.F.K. INTERNATIONAL AIRPORT

J.F.K. International Airport is by far the largest of the city's airports, has good transportation links and is particularly popular for its links with Europe.

There are a number of public transportation options to get to and from JFK. Most people take the AirTrain, which drops off at Jamaica Station - here NYC buses and three subway lines run to the rest of Manhattan.

The Aitrain also goes to Howard Beach Station where the A train and the Q11 bus run. The whole trip from the airport to Manhattan using the Airtrain and subway takes about 1 hour (10 minutes on the AirTrain itself) and costs $7.75 (including a transfer to the subway or bus).

The NYC Airporter bus is another option and departs every 30 minutes, costing $16.

If you want to take a taxi, JFK offers a flat fare of $52, plus tolls and tip to anywhere in Manhattan.

Uber, Lyft and other ride sharing services also operate from the airport but may be more expensive than cabs as they may not offer a flat rate.

# Rail Services

If you are travelling domestically, taking a train to NYC can be a great idea. Penn Station is conveniently located in Midtown West where you can easily find public transportation to anywhere in Manhattan. Amtrak, LIRR, and NJ Transit lines all run through Penn Station.

Grand Central Terminal is another hub, however, it is most often used by commuters. The lines run north to upstate New York and Connecticut.

# Bus Services

Buses are often the cheapest way of travelling domestically. Many go back and forth between the Port Authority, such as Greyhound, MegaBus, and Bolt buses. There are also buses that run more local routes (e.g. Boston or Washington D.C.) that are very inexpensive and depart from Chinatown. Booking these in advance is important as they can often be full.

# Transportation in NYC

*Transportation in NYC is abundant and extremely important in getting around. You will rarely have to wait more than five minutes for either a subway, a bus or a taxi during normal hours.*

## Subway

The subway is the preferred method of getting around the city for many. It runs 24 hours a day, with limited service late in the evenings and on the weekends. That means that not all lines operate between midnight and 6:00am.

Although the same did not hold true in the 1970s, the subways now are relatively safe. During weekdays in Manhattan they remain populated until about midnight. Also, many plain clothed and uniformed policemen are in and around the subway system.

That said, keeping an eye on your belongings in crowded subway 'cars' (the New York term for subway carriages) is always a good idea. It is smart to put your bag between your legs or on your stomach as pick pockets do operate – always keep your belongings in front of you.

The subway is structured by number/letter and color. This is both simple and complicated. Within Manhattan, most trains of the same color run on the same line, however, one or two of them will run express routes. Express route trains do not stop at all stations. This is important to know, because if you simply get on a train of the right color, it may not stop where you want to get off.

The good news is that every time you enter the subway system, you have as many free rides and transfers until you exit. Thus, if you do make a mistake, simply get off at the next stop, take the stairs to the opposite platform, and go in the other direction. However, it is important to keep an eye out for the Local/Express trains and understand how to properly read the subway map.

Before entering through the ticket barriers, be sure to know whether you are going generally North (Uptown) or South (Downtown). This is because many local stops (and some express stops) have one entrance on one side of the street for Uptown trains and another entrance on the other side of the street for Downtown trains. If the station entrance is Uptown or Downtown only, this will be clearly marked at the entrance to the station.

## Understanding the Subway Map:

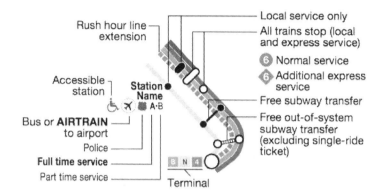

On the subway map you will see all of the stops and the lines which are clearly indicated by their colors. On the map, black dots indicate that there is a stop, but only local trains stop there.

White dots indicate that both local and express service trains stop there. If a white or black dot covers multiple lines on the map, a transfer between those lines is available. A black line

connecting two small dots means a transfer available, but it usually requires a longer walk through an underground passageway.

## Express Trains and Local Trains:

Next to each stop number, you will see a small number or letter combination – this indicates which of the colored trains stop at a given station.

For example, on the 1/2/3 line, next to Penn Station it shows that all three trains stop there. However, at 28th street, only the 1 is listed. This is because the 1 is local and the 2 and 3 are express trains.

Here are the express/local trains for each line:
- A/C/E: C – Local; A/E – Express
- 1/2/3: 1 – Local; 2/3 – Express
- 4/5/6: 6 – Local; 4/5 – Express
- N/Q/R: R – Local; Q/N – Express
- B/D/F/M: M – Local; BDF - Express

## Pricing:

Subway fares in New York are a flat rate no matter how far you travel and for a major city are relatively affordable. They are cheaper than London's fares, for example, but more expensive than Paris'.

Subway fares are loaded onto MetroCards, which can be used both on subways and local buses.

A metro card costs $1 and you can then add subway rides to it, or cash. If you are on a budget it is important to be economical. Here is the breakdown of pricing:

• Pay-Per Ride
- Buy as many rides as you want
- A single MetroCard ride costs $2.75
- Load up to $80 on the card at a time. An 11% bonus credit is added to your card when you load at least $5.50 in one transaction.

• Single Ride ticket
- $3.00 for one ride. No transfers. Valid for 2 hours.

•7-Day Unlimited - $31.00
- Unlimited subway and local bus rides until midnight.

• 30-Day Unlimited - $116.50
- Unlimited subway and local bus rides until midnight.

•7-Day Express Bus Plus - $57.25
- Unlimited express bus, local bus, and subway rides until midnight.

Important to note:
• If you are planning on fewer than 13 rides in a week or 48 rides in a month, then the Pay-Per-Ride rates (with the 11% bonus) are the best value for you. Otherwise, you should either get a 7-Day Unlimited or 30-Day Unlimited card.
• Up to three children, 44 inches tall and under, ride for free when accompanied by a fare-paying adult on subways and local buses.
• Infants (under two years of age) ride express buses free if the child sits on the lap of the accompanying adult.
• On unlimited cards, there is a time limit that goes into effect after one swipe. Thus, you cannot buy an unlimited card for two people, and swipe one person right after the other. A grace period of about 20 minutes goes into effect after one swipe to ensure that everyone has his or her own card.

• If you are using Pay Per Ride, up to four people can share the same card. Simply swipe the Metrocard for the number of people riding and then walk through the turnstile consecutively. Alternatively, each person can swipe and walk through and then pass the card back.
• Not all stations have people working to help you. There are automated machines where you can purchase tickets. These are pretty reliable.
• The direction you are going will be indicated by a sign that usually says "Downtown" or "Uptown" or the last name of the stop of that line.
• Upon exiting there are usually multiple stairwells that lead to corners dictated by North/South/East/West. If you are meeting someone ask them which exit to use or you could find yourself making a 5-minute walk around the block.

# Buses

While buses in NYC are available, most people prefer the subway in Manhattan due to the traffic. Subways run primarily up and down town, while buses frequently run across town. The fares are the same as they are for the subway, and you can transfer at certain locations without paying an extra fee. The exception to this are the express buses for long-distance trips – here the fare is not $2.75 per ride, but $6.50.

# Cycling

Cycling as a form of transportation in NYC has become much more popular in recent years. Bike lanes are available on most streets and many people use them. For the most part, the roads in Manhattan are perfectly flat, with no hills. It is perfectly acceptable to tour NYC by bike but you should be advised that cab drivers, NYC cyclists, and pedestrians, operate at their own pace and can make it a threatening place to ride.

Make sure you are going the right way on one-way streets, stay in the bike lanes if they are available, and be vigilant about your surroundings.

There are a number of bike rental options throughout the city and there is the option to use the Citi Bike program. You can get 24 hours of rides for unlimited 30-minute trips for $9.95 or 7 days of rides for $25.00. Trips over 30 minutes in length cost extra. Although the Citi Bike program allows more flexibility, most visitors to the city will still choose to use the subway as it is far better value and less tiring.

# Cabs

There is always the option to grab a cab in NYC. You will see them... everywhere.

All cabs have lights on the top of them. If the light is on, there is a vacancy. If the light is off, they already have people in their cabs. To hail a cab, you simply wave them over. They will pull to the side of the street and when you hop in they will ask your destination.

Taxi rides are metered, which means both time and distance affect the rate. If there is a lot of traffic, rates will be higher. Cabs are technically not allowed to turn you down but late at night, or at the end of long shifts, many will reject giving rides if they are not in the direction that they are going.

The base rate of a cab fare is $2.50 plus 50 cents per 1/5 of a mile, or 50 cents per 1 minute in slow traffic or when the vehicle is stopped. Passengers must pay all tolls and surcharges.

A surcharge of at least $0.80 is added to each fare, and there may be a peak time surcharge of $1 too depending on when you travel. There is no charge for extra passengers or luggage.

NYC cabs take cash and cards for all amounts, but individual bills over $20 are generally not accepted. A tip of at least 15% will be expected in addition to the fare shown on the meter.

One thing to be careful of is gypsy or illegal cabs. These are black cars that will pull over when you are trying to hail taxis and they may try and charge you a flat rate. Most of these cars are illegal and may overcharge you. It is better to stay with the yellow cab service.

Other popular options are Uber and Lyft - these are smartphone applications that allow you to alert a cab to your location, and it will pick you up. You connect your credit card to the application and the payment processes automatically. Get $20 of free credit for Uber by using our exclusive link at www.uber.com/invite/uberindependentguides.

# Accommodation

Like the city itself, housing and accommodation options are varied and widespread.

Accommodation in New York City is among the most expensive in the world. In 2013, average daily room rates were $290/night.

The luxury hotels have numerous rooms that go above and beyond $600/night. Most of these hotels are indeed expensive, but will give you the space and luxury of a king.

More standard hotels can be found for under $300 per night. Hostels and budget accommodation can run as low as $50 per night, but seldom below that.

If you are booking last minute (or up to 7 days before arrival), try Hotel Tonight. This is available as an app download and can get you up to 40% off the standard price of rooms as it sells last-minute inventory only. Our promo code "GDACOSTA4" will also save you an additional $25.

Airbnb is another option for travelers, where you can rent out a room in someone's house or an entire apartment.

Although you are not necessarily going to pay less money, if you do careful research you may be able to find a nice apartment that more closely mirrors NYC life for a similar price for a hotel room. If you are going to be touring for more than a week this is a good option to consider if you are interested in staying in a more residential neighborhood, as opposed to being among only tourists. It also allows you to cook your own meals and save a bit of money that way. If you will be using Airbnb, our exclusive link will give you a discount of at least $25 - it is www.airbnb.co.uk/c/gdacosta16.

Lastly, there is couch surfing – a free, or minimal opportunity – orchestrated online to, quite literally, crash on someone's couch. While this may be a viable option, one thing to note is that space is perceived very differently to New Yorkers than to most other people. As in, New Yorkers are used to less space; much less of it. If you are a person who needs a lot of privacy and quiet, this is not the best option.

In this guide we have included a look at accommodation options in our City Guide section, along with popular hotspots and places to eat. This allows you to find a neighborhood you like, and then find local places to stay and dine.

# Top 10 Attractions

*Your itinerary will largely be determined by how long your stay is. It takes a lifetime to do everything in NYC, so here are our top ten things that we believe should be prioritized.*

*Each attraction lists opening hours, admission prices and other important details. Subway listings state the train line you should get and where to get off.*

## 1. Metropolitan Museum of Art

 Adults: $25, Seniors: $17, Students: $12, Child Under 12: Free (with an adult)

 6 train to 86th Street; 4/6 trains to 77th Street

 212-731-1498

 www.metmuseum.org

 Daily from 10:00am to 5:30pm.

Known locally as The Met, this museum is the largest art museum in the United States and has been in operation since 1872. There are 17 curatorial departments and the permanent collection has over two million works from all over the world. The outside architecture alone is worth seeing. The walls, stairs and columns are influenced by Beaux-Arts architecture of neoclassical style.

The Met is situated along Central Park, and the inside boasts massive glass walls into which natural light floods. Additionally, there is a Roof Garden which exhibits art, has a café and bar, and some of the best views of Central Park and the skyline in Manhattan.

The temporary exhibitions at The Met are usually very well done and should be looked into before going. As the place is enormous, it is best to go in with a plan so as not to get lost.

# 2. Times Square

 Free    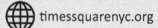 timessquarenyc.org     1/2/3/7/A/C/E/ N/Q/R/S trains to Times Square

Times Square is a tourist's mecca; it is a commercial intersection that goes from West 42nd to West 47th Street and convenes at Broadway.

It is Times Square that has given NYC the reputation as the 'City of Lights', and it is certainly a must-see on any itinerary.

At most times of the day and night this intersection is flooded with people. There are many tourists, as well as people in the business and entertainment industry.

The area is also known as the Theater District, as the surrounding streets house many of the city's musicals and plays.

The TKTS booth at the northern end of Times Square is a good place to go for discounted theater tickets: sometimes you have to wait in line and you may not have every show to choose from, but there can be discounts of up to 50%.

Times Square is home to Planet Hollywood, M&M's World, the Disney Store, and The Hard Rock Café are other popular tourist spots. We recommend experiencing Times Square during the nighttime to get the full effect of the lights and atmosphere.

# 3. Central Park

 N/R/W to 59th Street; 2/3 to Central Park North/110th Street; B/C to 110th Street, 103rd Street, 96th Street, 86th Street, 81st Street, and 72nd Street; A/B/C/D/1 to 59th Street/Columbus Circle

 www.centralparknyc.org

 Daily from 6:00am to 1:00am

Central Park is a bit of an enigma; it is the antithesis of Manhattan, yet it blends so seamlessly into the island that it would be impossible to imagine the city without it.

It is a reminder to its residents of the nature and serenity that exists in so much of the world that is so rarely seen in this city.

As the weather gets nice in the city, New Yorkers flock to the grassy fields in droves. For children, it's an alternative to a backyard; youth sporting events and practices may take place.

For young adults, it's a venue for a pickup, and to toss a Frisbee around. For athletes, it's the best free training ground available. And for all New Yorkers, it's a gorgeous place of refuge and relaxation.

At certain times of the year free concerts are also held in the park - and other special events are regularly held here.

There are many different ways to explore Central Park, and many different places to see. Rowing boats are available to rent on the lake.

There are also several places to rent bikes to take on the 6-mile loop around the whole park, or you can get a horse carriage ride ($54 plus tip for 20 minutes) or Pedi cab ride. Alternatively, you can always walk.

# 4. High Line

 L to 14th Street; A/C/E to 14th or 34th Street; 1/2/3 to 14th or 34th Street

 Daily. From 7:00am to 7:00pm from December to March; from 7:00am to 10:00pm from April to May, October & November; and from 7:00am to 11:00pm from June to September.

 www.thehighline.org

The High Line is a new addition to NYC, having opened in 2009. This linear park was built on an elevated section of a railroad called the West Side Line. It extends from Gansevoort Street to 34th Street and is best experienced by walking from one end to the other.

It passes under the Chelsea Market – a sizable food hall on 15th Street – where many visitors break for a meal, and it is situated over the various art galleries that Chelsea is famed for. Unique to the High Line are the interesting plants and landscaping that grow over the old train tracks. Additionally, temporary art installations change throughout the year.

# 5. MoMA

 E/M to 53rd Street; B/D/F/M to Rockefeller Center

 Saturdays to Thursday from 10:30am to 5:00pm. Fridays from 10:30am to 8:00pm.

 www.moma.org

 Adults: $25, Seniors: $18, Students: $14, Free for children 16 and under

 11 W 53rd St, New York

 212-708-9400

The Museum of Modern Art (MoMA) is renowned for housing some of the most important modern art in the world.

Though it has been in operation since the early 1900s, renovations in 1983 and 2002 have doubled its original gallery size and have made the place an open and modern structure.

The permanent collections are considered some of the best in world with famous artists such as Paul Cezanne, Marc Chagall, Salvador Dali, Frida Kahlo, Claude Monet, Henri Matisse, Andy Warhol, Pablo Picasso, Jackson Pollock, Vincent Van Goh, and countless others.

Temporary collections are usually highly regarded and appropriately timed. Additionally, there are numerous film exhibitions and events held throughout the year. For those interested in contemporary art, the MoMA is an excellent place to spend the better half of a day.

# 6. Brooklyn Bridge

 4/5/6 to Brooklyn Bridge; N/R to City Hall; A/C High Street; F to York Street

 24/7

 http://www.nyc.gov/html/dot/html/infrastructure/brooklyn-bridge.shtml

 Free

 11 W 53rd St, New York

The Brooklyn Bridge is a unique fixture not just in New York, but also in the world. The hybrid cable-stayed/suspension bridge was completed in 1883 and it connects lower Manhattan to Dumbo and Brooklyn Heights.

The bridge itself is an architectural masterpiece, and unlike the two other bridges that connect Manhattan to Brooklyn – the Manhattan and the Williamsburg bridges – a subway does not run across, making it a quieter and more peaceful place to marvel at the lower Manhattan skyline - if you ignore the traffic below, that is.

Walking from Manhattan to Brooklyn you can make your way to Brooklyn Bridge Park, which provides spectacular views of Manhattan at Sunset. The length of the bridge is 1.1 miles (and 1.8 kilometers) long.

# 7. Tenement Museum

 F to Delancey Street; J/M/Z to Essex Street

 Available with reservation only.

 www.tenement.org

 Adults: $25, Seniors and Students: $20

 103 Orchard Street

 877-975-3786

The Tenement Museum is an unassuming institution on the Lower East Side that successfully brings the history of immigrants living in NYC between 1869 and 1935 to life. For those interested in history, this is a prime spot to go, and for those not so interested, this is the place that may spark your curiosity.

The museum is only seen through guided tours. While initially it may seem unappealing to some, the staff are incredibly well versed, patient, and engaging. They offer a few different kinds of tours that detail certain aspects of immigrant life – from shop ownership to sweatshop workers.

They give walking tours of the neighborhood, and have actors that act as the residents of the tenement on Orchard Street. The tours go through recreated tenements and shops that accurately replicate the style of the time.

Additionally, the museum has a free bookshop with an interesting collection of books about or based in NYC, and various other NYC related trinkets.

# 8. 9/11 Memorial Complex

 A/C to Chambers or Fulton; E to World Trade Center; 1/2/3 to Chamber Streets; R to Cortlandt Street; 1/R to Rector Street

 See description.

 www.911memorial.org

 See description.

 180 Greenwich Street

 212 312-8800

The events of September 11, 2001 greatly changed NYC, and its residents have not forgotten them. In 2011, this memorial opened. Michael Arad and Peter Walker's design, "Reflecting Absence" was chosen and construction began in 2006.

The memorial consists of two one-acre pools with the largest man-made waterfalls in the United States. The victims' names are inscribed on bronze plates that are attached to the walls of the pools. Trees fill the rest of the 6 acres of the plaza. The memorial is respectful, peaceful and breathtaking.

In 2014, the Museum section opened to the public. The exhibits have numerous images, artifacts, and oral histories of the people who were killed. We think it is the best museum we have seen in any city around the world.

Finally, also located on-site is One World Trade Center, the tallest building in the US. At 1,776 feet tall, this building dominates NYC's skyline. On floors 100 to 102 you can visit the observation deck.

**Memorial** – Open: Daily from 7:30am to 9:00pm. Free Admission.

**Museum** – Open: Sun to Thurs from 9:00am to 8:00pm; Fri to Sat from 9:00am to 9:00pm. Free Admission: Tuesdays after 5:00pm. Other Days: Adults: $24, Seniors, Veterans and Students: $18, Ages 7 to 17: $15, Children 6 and under: Free.

**Observatory** – Open: Daily from 9:00am to 8:00pm. Adults: $32, Seniors $30 and Children $26.

# 9. Top of the Rock

 B/D/F/M to 47-50th Streets; E/M to 50th Street.

 www.topoftherocknyc.com

 30 Rockefeller Plaza

 See description.

 Adult: $30, Child: $28, Senior: $20; Two visits in one day: Adult: $45, Child: $30.

 212-698-2000

Although the Empire State Building has views of the city, the experience of going to the Top of Rockefeller Plaza yields the best views of anywhere in the NYC area, in our opinion.

Upon entering, you will go through a mezzanine exhibit detailing the story of Rockefeller Center and the Top of the Rock. Interactive components, such as the 'beam walk', put you in the shoes of the people who constructed the building. After a short video you will enter the "sky shuttle" that will take you to the top.

At the top is an indoor space with comfortable seating and floor-to-ceiling windows where you can enjoy remarkable views. An outdoor space is also available on several levels. Binoculars are available outdoors to see NYC through glass panels. Finally, a photographer is always on site to take photographs.

# 10. The Cloisters

 A to 190th Street; 1 to 191st Street

 Daily. March to October from 10:00am to 5:15pm. November to February from 10:00am to 4:45pm.

 www.metmuseum.org

 Adults: $25, Seniors: $17, Students: $12, Children under 12: Free

 99 Margaret Corbin Drive

 212-923-3700

The location of The Cloisters makes it a difficult spot for most tourists to hit, but if you have extra time, it is certainly a sight to see.

Located in the northern tip of Manhattan in Fort Tyron Park in the neighborhood of Washington Heights, this is an extension of The Met. What's more, if you visit The Met on the same day, admission to The Cloisters is free.

The museum exhibits art, architecture, and artifacts from Medieval Europe.

What makes it such a unique place is the setting; it is situated on top of a hill, which overlooks the Hudson River. The landscaping was done in a curatorial way with horticultural information used from medieval archives to create a representative botanical experience.

If you venture up, make sure it is a beautiful day, as that will greatly enhance the experience. Fort Tyron Park, created by John D. Rockefeller, Jr. in 1917 is a scenic and quiet place to take a walk to escape the hectic nature of Manhattan.

# Neighbourhood Guides

*Now it's time to take a look at New York City by taking a look at each neighborhood individually. New York City is more than just Manhattan, so this section covers the main island as well as all outer boroughs.*

As we look through each neighborhood, we have included a brief description and history of the area, a look at accommodation options, along with popular hotspots and places to eat. Organizing the guide in this manner allows you to find a neighborhood you like, and then find local places to stay and dine.

In this section, where subway transportation is listed, we state the train number/letter followed by where you should get off. E.g. "1 to 125th Street" means you should take the '1' train to the '125th Street' stop.

Each attraction, restaurant and accommodation listed features a fact sheet with symbols, the key below helps to explain what each of these symbols means.

 Nearest subway stop

 Opening Hours

 Address

 Website

 Entry price

 Phone number

# Harlem

*Harlem is most often associated with the Harlem Renaissance – an era during the 1920s and 1930s in the United States when African-American cultural expression flourished and rose to prominence. While the neighborhood has certainly changed, it holds onto its history and identity as one of the most progressive black neighborhoods in the United States by preserving some of the establishments and practices that brought it critical acclaim.*

After World War II and the Great Depression, Harlem saw a significant economic downfall. Race riots and protests, ultimately contributed to the Civil Rights movement in the United States, and Harlem became known as a poor and dangerous neighborhood.

Since the 2000s many renovations have taken place and the neighborhood is growing economically again, and changing at a fast rate. While it was reported in 2000 that 77% of the population was black, this was a significant decrease from 98% in 1950. Over the past few years

Harlem has continued to get more and more diverse.

Iconic venues such as the Apollo Theater, that first saw people like Ella Fitzgerald and James Brown are still up and running. However, now they are integrated amidst the newer cultural institutions such as celebrity Chef's, Marcus Samuelsson's, rendition of old comfort-food classics.

As far as safety is concerned this is still a touchy subject. Although many people feel perfectly safe in Harlem, you do have to remember that this is a very large area and

therefore there are all kinds of different people and safety varies. There are definitely still some very rough parts of the area, particularly around the housing projects along 8th Avenue and between 130th and 145th Streets.

On the other hand, there are very many churchgoers in Harlem too, and the area contains some of the city's most beautiful architecture. The most frequented parts of Harlem by tourists are based around 125th Street. Use your common sense as you walk around, as you would anywhere else in the city.

# Attractions

## The Studio Museum in Harlem

 2/3 to 125th Street; A/B/C/D to 125th Street

 Adults: $7, Students & seniors: $3, Under 12s: Free. Free for all on Sundays.

 Thursdays and Fridays from 12:00pm to 9:00pm; Saturdays from 10:00am to 6pm; Sundays from 12:00pm to 6:00pm.

 144 W 125th Street

 www.studiomuseum.org

The Studio Museum in Harlem is dedicated to exhibiting contemporary African-American art. The museum was established in 1968, beginning in a rented loft, and has grown to be one of the most notable of its kind. The permanent collection has over 2,000 works. The museum also has an Artists-in-Residence program, which has supported over 100 emerging artists of African or Latino descent.

## El Museo del Barrio

 4/6 to 103rd Street

 Adults: $9, Students & seniors: $5; Unders 12: Free. Free for all every third Saturday of the month.

 Wed to Sat 11:00am to 6:00pm, Sun midday to 5:00pm

 1230 Fifth Avenue

 www.elmuseo.org

Often referred to as simply, "El Museo," this museum has transformed from a Fire Station to a space that stores approximately 8,500 pieces of pre-Columbian works and artifacts, as well as contemporary art.

The inspiration came about during the Nuyorican Movement – a cultural movement during the Civil Rights Era when Puerto Ricans living in NYC began to demand equal rights and treatment.

The museum has continually fought for funding, and a Frida Kahlo exhibit in 2002 increased its popularity and profitability. A partnership with the Museum of the City of New York allows you to visit both museums for the admission price of one.

# Cotton Club

 1 to 125th Street;  See description.

 Swing dance on Mon from 8:00pm; Dinner on Thurs from 8:00pm and Sat from 9:00pm; Jazz & Blues night on Fridays; Gospel show weekends 12:00 and 14:30.

 656 W 125th Street  www.cottonclub-newyork.com

From 1923 to 1935, the Cotton Club was NYC's premier nightclub. Although it was a whites-only venue, many black performers – Louis Armstrong, Ethel Waters, Billie Holiday, to name a few – performed there.

The club closed in 1936 as a result of race riots and boycotts surrounding the racial prejudice. It reopened later that year in Midtown until 1940 when it proved too expensive to run.

In the 1970s they built a replica of the original Cotton Club, which still stands today.

Swing dance: $25; Dinner: $56.50; Fridays night: $20 cover; Gospel show: $43.50

# Apollo Theater

 A/B/C/D to 125th Street;
2/3 to 125th Street

 Prices vary per show

 Tours: Mondays, Tuesdays, Thursdays, & Fridays at 11:00am, 1:00pm and 3:00pm; Wednesdays to 11:00am; Weekends at 11:00am & 1:00pm

 253 W 125th Street

 www.apollotheater.org

The Apollo was originally built as a Burlesque Theater in 1913 to 1914 as a whites-only venue.

In 1934, Sidney Cohen reopened the venue, with the hope of catering to black musical artists and audience members. While some nights were open to white performers, the notable artists that performed there were Duke Ellington, Sam Cooke, Aretha Franklin, Otis Redding, Ray Charles, and countless others.

After the 1960s the theater saw a decline, and after a few different owners, it was purchased by the State of New York. It's registered as a NYC Landmark and draws 1.3 million visitors a year.

Historic tours last one hour and offered 2 to 3 times daily, except for Wednesday when they offer a special package with tickets for the Amateur Night, and tickets must be purchased in advance. They don't offer individual tours, although individuals can join group tours if there is a demand. Tours are $16 per person on weekdays and $18 on weekends. Performances take place regularly.

## Schomburg Center for Research in Black Culture

 2/3 to 135th Street  Free entry

 Mondays, Thursdays and Fridays from 10:00am to 6:00pm; Tuesdays and Wednesdays from 10:00am to 8:00pm. Closed on weekends.

 515 Malcolm X Boulevard  www.nypl.org/locations/schomburg

Although a Library may not be the first place you want to go as a tourist, the Schomburg Center for Research in Black Culture is unique and historically significant.

The Library opened in 1905 after Andrew Carnegie donated a hefty sum for 65 branch libraries to be built throughout the city. In the 1920s, black people were integrated into the staff and they held the first exhibition of African-American art in Harlem 1921.

African-American scholar Arturo Alfonso Schomburg donated and sold his enormous collection to be made available to the public in 1926. In 1942 an extension was built and the library underwent different leadership.

In 1980 the new Schomburg Center was founded, and the original building on 135th street was named a NYC Landmark. Since 1998 it's been considered the best Afrocentric artifact collection of any public library in the United States.

The Center has five divisions – Art and Artifacts, Research and References, Manuscripts and Archives and Rare Books, Moving Image and Recorded Sound, and Photographs and Prints. Additionally, there are readings, art exhibitions and theatrical events – all open to the public.

# Dining

## Make My Cake

 2/3 to 116th Street; B/C to 116th Street  212-932-0833

 Mon to Thurs from 8:00am to 8:00pm; Fridays from 8:00am to 9:00pm; Saturdays from 9:00am to 9:00pm; Sundays from 9:00am to 7:00pm

 121 Saint Nicholas Avenue  www.makemycake.com

For those with a sweet tooth, Make My Cake is likely to satisfy the craving. The bakery sells home-baked recipes of cakes, pies, cookies, breads, and cupcakes. It's known for its decadent Red Velvet Cake, a southern classic. The recipes are said to have derived from the owners southern Heritage.

# Red Rooster

 2/3 to 125th Street;
A/C/B/D to 125th Street   212-792-9001

 Mon to Fri 11:30am to 3:30pm & 4:30pm 10:30pm; Sat 10:00am to 3:00pm
& 4:30pm to 11:30pm; Sun 10:00am to 3:00pm & 4:30pm to 10:00pm

 310 Lenox Avenue   www.redroosterharlem.com

Named after a legendary Speakeasy in Harlem during the Prohibition Era, Andrew Chapman and Marcus Samuelsson opened this restaurant to celebrate Harlem's history and vibrant culture.

Samuelsson is an award-winning chef, cookbook author, and the youngest chef to receive two three-star ratings from the New York Times.

The menu boasts interesting adaptations to southern classics, as well as the dishes in their original form. Dishes like Macaroni and Cheese and Collard Greens ($18) and Barbeque Pork Chop ($27) embody some of the classic entrees. However, Ethiopian inspired dishes – Beef Kitfo ($14) and Teff Grits ($8) – can also be found amidst the menu.

A brunch menu is also available, as well as an eclectic cocktail menu. Sometimes the restaurant doubles as an art space.

## Dinosaur Bar-B-Que

 1 to 125th Street  212-694-1777

 Mondays to Thursdays from 11:30am to 11:00pm; Fridays to Saturdays from 11:30am to 12:00am; Sundays from 12:00pm to 10:00pm

 700 W 125th Street  www.dinosaurbarbque.com/menu-harlem

The concept and execution of this nationally acclaimed Bar-B-Que chain began in upstate New York during the 1980s by some motorcyclists. Throughout the 1990s and early 2000s, they have opened seven locations in five different states.

They've been named the country's best BBQ on Good Morning America and the chain is highly regarded by other commercial publications.

The atmosphere is fun and lively. There's often a considerable wait here, although most people think it's worth the while.

They're famed for their homemade BBQ sauce, which can be bought separately.

Many are fans of their Brisket and Pulled Pork Plates ($18 and $17) as well as their Creole Spiced Deviled Eggs ($4/$7/$13). Sandwiches will run you about $11 while plates are more in the range of $18. However, servings are big and can certainly be shared. They even have a Vegetarian Smoke Portobello ($12) and gluten free options are available so everyone can find something.

Finally, they have over 25 beers on tap.

## Sylvia's Restaurant

 2/3 to 125th Street  212-996-0660

 Mondays to Saturdays from 8:00am to 10:30pm; Sundays from 11:00am to 8:00pm

 328 Malcolm X Boulevard  www.sylviasrestaurant.com

Since 1962 when Sylvia Woods, dubbed "Queen of Soulfood", opened her restaurant it has become a neighborhood staple.

Many notable people have eaten at this establishment, including Bill Clinton, Nelson Mandela, Caroline Kennedy, Al Sharpton and others.

The menu has a wide range of breakfast and fried foods, from the classic Shrimp & Grits ($16) to Fried Chicken Legs ($11). It's famous for its Sunday Gospel Breakfast, serving Hot Cakes with Meats ($15-$18), cocktails, and rich desserts.

## The Cecil

 2/3 to 125th Street     212-996-0660

 Mon to Thur 5:30pm to 10:30pm; Fri 5:00pm to 11:00pm; Sat 11:00am to 3:00pm & 5:00pm to 11:00pm; Sun 11:00am to 3:00pm & 5:00pm to 11:00pm

 328 Malcolm X Boulevard     www.sylviasrestaurant.com

Richard Parsons, a businessman, and chef, Alexander Smalls, came together in 2013 to create what Esquire magazine called the best new restaurant in the country. The cuisine is a creative fusion of African, Asian, and American cuisines. The results are entrees like the Cinnamon Scented Fried Guinea Hen ($27) or a Pan Roasted Skuna Bay Salmon ($29). Most ingredients and products are found locally.

## Abyssinia Restaurant

 A/B/C to 135th Street; 2/3 to 135th Street     212-281-2673

 Daily from 12:00pm to 10:00pm

 268 W 135th Street     www.harlemethiopianfood.com

The owners of Abyssinia were Ethiopians that began selling Injera in bulk from their apartment 8 years ago – a rarity in NYC.

They originally only sold products to Ethiopians. Now they have a restaurant that serves up authentic Ethiopian fare to everyone.

With a large and growing Ethiopian population throughout the city, the reception has been positive.

The vegetable dishes, and meat and lentil stews, run from $12 to $15 per entrée, or you can get a combination platter and try them all. They also serve honey wine.

# Accommodation

## Aloft Harlem

 2/3 to 125th Street     646-248-1890

 248 Malcolm X Blvd     www.theinternationalcozyinn.com

Aloft Harlem is a newly renovated hotel with modern design and loft-inspired rooms. There is a bar, a pool table, free Wi-Fi, and free bottles of water for guests.

Many families visiting Columbia University opt to stay here, as it's just a short 10-minute walk away.

Most regard it as nothing all too special, but good value for the money.

Rooms are usually between $240 to $270 per night.

## The International Cozy Inn

 A/B/C/D to 125th Street; 2/3 to 125th Street     212-749-4000

 2296 Frederick Douglass Boulevard     www.aloftharlem.com

This hotel is a very quirky and unique option that is great for travelling with the family or a few friends.

There are different suite-style options available, each decorated with bright patterned betting, and some with kitchens and closed fireplaces.

If you're staying in NYC for a longer period of time and don't mind falling asleep to bright colors and somewhat unmatchable décor, this is a great option.

Prices range from $50 to $80 per person for a 4-person minimum suite, and move up from there.

## Sugar Hill Harlem Inn

 1 to 145th Street; A/C to 145th Street

 212-234-5432

 460 W 141st Street

 www.sugarhillharleminn.com

This Inn prides itself on being a historical mecca like no other. Sugar Hill was the neighborhood that housed a crowd of progressive museums during the Harlem Renaissance, and the owners here don't want you to forget it.

The Inn is situated in a Victorian Townhouse built in 1906. Although renovations in 2001 make it so the rooms are clean, well lit, and have running water, the Victorian designs remain true to their roots. The rooms are homey and named after famous Harlem artists, and there is a garden that can be enjoyed in the warmer months with a variety of plants.

Rooms range from $125 to $275 per night.

## Harlem YMCA

 2/3 to 135th Street; B/C to 135th Street

 212-912-2100

 180 West 135th Street

 www.ymcanyc.org/association/guest-rooms/harlemrooms

For those travelling on a strict budget, the Harlem YMCA is a good option for lodging. With complimentary luggage storage, a breakfast voucher, free Wi-Fi, and no curfew, this is an ideal place for young people who are constantly exploring. Additionally, a pool and gym are available for use. Rooms are $50/night per person.

# Upper West Side

*Located close to Columbia, the Upper West Side is known to be a residential place for the upwardly mobile cultural and intellectual crowd. Until the turn of the 20th century, the area was largely considered the countryside, as it had not been developed yet. However, with the development of the rail lines and public transportation, people began to settle in upper Manhattan.*

The first residents of the Upper West Side were largely African-Americans, many of whom were veterans of the Spanish-American War. Many scenes in the musical 'West Side Story' were filmed among the tenement streets, highlighting racial and gang tensions in the area.

After World War II, a combination of gay white men and young college graduates began populating the Upper West Side, gentrifying the neighborhood. Tenements were torn down and the now-multimillion dollar brownstones were built, as were a series of gigantic modern apartment buildings of

Donald Trump looking out on the Hudson River.

The area now is much whiter and more affluent, but minority populations still exist. It's a pleasant place to walk around – the sidewalks are wider, quieter, and you are rarely more than a short walk from Central Park.

## Attractions

### New York Historical Society

 A/B/C to 81st Street   Adults: $20, Seniors &military: $15, Students: $12, Ages 5-13: $6, Under 5: Free

 Tuesdays to Thursdays and Saturdays from 10:00am to 6:00pm; Fridays from 10:00am to 8:00pm; Sundays from 11:00am to 5:00pm

 170 Central Park West   www.nyhistory.org

In 1804, the New York Historical Society became New York's first museum. It has been at the current location since 1908, and is a great for those interested in American history. The institution is known for unique innovations, such as a two-year exhibit

held about slavery in New York, which began in 2005.

The exhibitions range from all topics throughout American history, but they are always well-researched and put together comprehensively. It has over 1.6 million works in

its permanent collections and has maintained its prestige as a premiere research institution. There is also a separate Children's Museum, with interactive exhibits and a theater.

Pay-as-you-wish from 6:00pm to 8:00pm on Fridays.

# American Museum of Natural History

 A/B/C to 81st Street

 Adults: $22, Students and seniors: $17, Children (2 to 12): $12.50

 Daily from 10:00am to 5:45pm

 www.amnh.org

 Central Park West at 79th Street

Often seen on signs and pamphlets as AMNH, the American Museum of Natural History. It comprises 27 interconnected buildings, as well as a planetarium and library.

With over 32 million specimens scattered throughout the 1,600,000 square feet this is one of the largest museums in the world and makes for a fascinating visit.

The three-dimensional exhibits make this an idyllic and enticing place for children to spend a few hours. However, the renowned curating makes for adult entertainment as well.

There are additional ticketed events, such as 2-D and 3-D film showings, as well as special exhibitions and limited-time offerings.

## American Folk Art Museum

 1 to 66th Street     Free

 Tuesdays to Thursdays from 11:30am to 7:00pm; Fridays from 12:00pm to 7:30pm; Saturdays from 11:30 to 7:00pm; Sundays from 12:00 to 6:00pm

 2 Lincoln Square     www.folkartmuseum.org

This museum praises self-taught artists and folk artists from the around the United States. Since 1961, the museum has continuously grown and experienced a rise in acclaim. It has over 5,000 objects from the 18th century and 7,000 items of the entire collection have been given as gifts. The temporary exhibitions usually focus on the self-taught artists, which results in unique and innovative visual pieces of work.

## Beacon Theater

 1/2/3 to 72nd Street     212-465-6500

 2124 Broadway     www.beacontheatre.com

The Beacon Theater was initially a deluxe movie palace for films and vaudeville. It opened in 1929 but was bought out in 1974 to become a music venue. It has hosted countless famous artists such as the Grateful Dead, the Allman Brothers Band, and served as a venue for other events.

The neo-Grecian architecture makes it a place to marvel at while walking to your seat and enjoying the music.

Renovations in 2009 revamped the cleanliness and utility of the venue while maintaining its authentic appeal. Big musical artist and groups perform here on a regular basis and it is truly a sight to be seen.

# Lincoln Center

 1 to 66th Street

 Adults: $18, Students (under 30): $18

 Tours offered daily between 10:30am and 4:00pm

 10 Lincoln Center Plaza      http://lc.lincolncenter.org/

Lincoln Center is a well-renowned complex with various facilities relating to the performance arts.

Some of the most notable performance spaces include Avery Fisher Hall, home to the New York Philharmonic, the Metropolitan Opera House, home to the Metropolitan Opera, the Julliard School, and Jazz at Lincoln Center, a premier jazz venue.

The entire institution is the world's largest presenter of performing arts and offers over 5,000 programs throughout the year. Numerous events are offered daily.

# Dining
## Alice's Tea Cup

 1/2/3 to 72nd Street; B/C to 72nd Street

 518-889-9344

 Daily 8:00am to 8:00pm

 102 West 73rd Street

 www.alicesteacup.com

This shop, self-dubbed "New York City's most whimsical tea house!" plays off of the novel and film, Alice in Wonderland, in every way.

With three locations throughout the city, they have mastered the art of scone baking and tea making, and have expanded the menu to include other meals.

Whether you want a simple scone and tea (including a vegan one) or a decadent meal, this place will satisfy all cravings.

Their extensive breakfast menu includes things like Wonderland Waffles ($12) or Alice's Florentine – Sautéed spinach and poached eggs on top of a buttermilk scone ($15).

They also offer a range of sandwiches and salads, but most people come for the baked goods.

# Absolute Bagels

 1 to Cathedral Parkway      212-932-2052

 Daily from 6:00am to 9:00pm

 2788 Broadway           www.absolutebagels.com

As most New Yorkers will know, a cheap unassuming awning atop a storefront that serves bagels is generally a good sign. This old tradition is a sacred one in NYC, and a modernized atmosphere is seldom seen in correspondence with the quality. In all of NYC, Absolute Bagels is one of the best.

There is often a line wrapped around the corner, so getting there before your hunger sets in is a pretty good idea. On Saturday and Sunday mornings it can be especially crowded.

The line does move pretty quickly and there are a wide range of both bagels and toppings (including various cream cheeses) to choose from ($3 to $8).

There is very limited seating but Riverside Park is just a five-minute walk towards the river and a scenic place for a picnic on a nice day.

# Boulud Sud

 1/2 to 66th Street      212-595-1313

 Mon to Wed 11:30am-2:30pm & 5:00-11:00pm; Thurs and Fri 11:00am-3:00pm & 5:00-11:30pm; Saturdays 11:00-3:00pm & 5:00pm-11:30pm; Sundays from 11:00am to 3:00pm & 5:00pm to 10:00pm

 20 West 64th Street     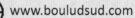 www.bouludsud.com

For those seeking a fine dining experience Boulud Sud is a good option. Famous Chef Daniel Boulud's menu features Mediterranean-inspired dishes with an emphasis on grilled fish, lamb, and fresh vegetables.

The dinner menu features items like Kale and Harissa Shakshoula, with potatoes, goat cheese, and a soft-cooked hen egg ($19) as well as Za'atar grilled Mediterranean Sea Bass ($32).

Additionally, the restaurant offers a pre-theater prix fixe menu served from 5:00pm to 7:00pm, Monday to Saturday. For $60, you can get an appetizer, entrée, and dessert.

## Gennaro

 1/2/3 to 96th Street     212-665-5348

 Mondays to Thursdays from 5:00pm to 10:30pm; Fridays to Sundays 5:00pm to 11:00pm.

 665 Amsterdam Avenue     www.gennaronyc.com

This cash-only Italian restaurant is more walk than talk. The ambience is relaxed and the menu is straightforward. However, what it lacks in complexity and innovation it makes up for in flavor.

The cuisine is classic Italian, using high-end ingredients, and relying on flavor more than creativity. Prices range from a basic pasta with tomato sauce ($12) to the homemade veal ravioli in tomato cream sauce ($18). The rest of entrees are largely meat based ($17 to $24) with a few seafood options mixed in.

## Toms Restaurant

 1 to 116th Street

 Sun to Wed from 6:00am to 1:30am; Thurs to Sat - 24 hours

 2880 Broadway

 212-864-6137

 tomsrestaurant.net

If you recognize the awning of Tom's Restaurant, don't doubt yourself. This family owned restaurant from the 1940s is famed for its appearance as Monk's Diner, the regular meeting spot for the characters on the show Seinfeld.

While the food here is nothing to write home about, the experience is worthwhile.

It's a classic old-style diner with various omelets breakfast options and sandwiches ($8 to $12).

Many people, including the local college students come here for high calorie snacks like French Fries, and their true specialties, the giant malted milk shakes ($6).

With reasonable prices, it's a good place to go for to a relaxed atmosphere.

# Accommodation

## Astor on the Park Hotel

 B/C to Cathedral Parkway

 465 Central Park West

 646-368-8939

 www.astoronpark.com

This budget hotel, while on the northern tip of the Upper West Side, is nicely situated right next to Central Park. With 112 furnished rooms with a small kitchenette, it's a good affordable option for those who don't need luxury service. The rooms, small and bland, are well-kept, and get the job done. Rooms start at around $100 per night. Wi-Fi is not included.

## Jazz on the Park

 B/C to 103rd Street or 110th Street

 36 West 106 Street

 212-932-1600

 www.astoronpark.com

Another solid budget option can be found at Jazz on the Park. This hostel has private and shared rooms from $45 to $150. A coffee shop is onsite, and outdoor terraces and a basement with regular events makes this a good place to meet others, if travelling alone. Free lockers, storage, maps, towels, and house keeping are included, and coin-operated washing machines are on site as well.

## NYLO

 1 to 79th Street

 2178 Broadway

 212-362-1100

 www.nylohotels.com/nyc

This 4-star hotel dubs itself as embodying "signature urban, industrial design with the energy, color and fashions of New York's Jazz Era." They pride themselves on offering the most comfortable beds on the market, and most rooms have large open windows providing great views of the surrounding area. Rooms range from $500 to $700 per night.

# Upper East Side

*Whereas the Upper West Side is known for the affluent families, the residents of the Upper East Side work primarily downtown in the commercial and financial industries. As one of the most affluent neighborhoods in NYC, it provides well-kept streets to roam and wander.*

Unlike most neighborhoods, the Upper East Side has always been inhabited by the people in the upper echelons of society.

As the area turned from farmland to mansions beside Central Park, people like Andrew Carnegie, Henry Clay Frick, and the Rockefellers were some of the first inhabitants. The only remaining mansion is Gracie Mansion, which has been the home of most NYC mayors since 1942.

The population now is mostly white, with more Jews and Republicans than most of the rest of the areas in NYC. A number of cultural institutions and museums are home to the Upper East Side and all offer something new and interesting.

## Attractions

### Frick Collection

Henry Frick was a famous art collector who moved to New York in 1905 and leased the Vanderbilt house at 640 Fifth Avenue. When he did so, a lot of his artwork came with him.

The museum today is in Frick's former residence and many of the pieces of artwork are supposedly arranged in their original formation.

 6 to 68th Street

 Tuesdays to Saturdays 10:00am to 6:00pm; Sundays 11:00am to 5:00pm

 1 E 70th Street

 www.frick.org

 Adults: $20, Over 65s: $15, Students: $10, Under 10s: Not admitted; Sun 11am to 1pm: pay-as-you-wish

# 92nd Street Y

 6 to 96th Street     212-415-5500

 1395 Lexington Avenue     www.92y.org

Having begun in 1874 as the Young Men's Hebrew Association, the 92nd Street Y has adapted to a cultural institution that serves various races, faiths, and ethnic groups. The venue hosts a wide range of programs – lectures, concerts, discussions, dances, readings, screenings, and others. Famous people such as Rachel Maddow and Ira Glass have been guests in events in the past. Check the schedule for events.

# Solomon R. Guggenheim Museum

 4/5/6 to 86th Street     Adults: $16, Students & seniors: $14, Under 12s: Free; Sat 5:45pm to 7:45pm pay-as-you-wish

 Sundays to Wed, and Fridays from 10:00am to 5:45pm; Saturdays from 10:00am to 7:45pm

 1071 5th Avenue     www.guggenheim.org/new-york

In operation since 1939, the Guggenheim Museum has been known for housing some of the most respected and well-known contemporary art.

The building itself is a magnificent piece of artwork. Designed by Frank Lloyd Wright, it is cylindrical, and wider at the top than it is the bottom. There is a ramp, which wraps around creating a walking coil.

The structure of the museum lends to displaying artwork in a particular, and often chronological, way.

There are permanent collections, but it's best known for the larger exhibitions that take up the majority of the space.

# Metropolitan Museum of Art

 6 to 86th Street; 4/6 to 77th Street

 Adults: $25, Seniors (Over 65): $17, Students: $12, Children (under 12): Free

 Sundays to Thursdays from 10:00am to 5:30pm; Fridays to Saturdays from 10:00am to 9:00pm

 1000 Fifth Avenue

 www.metmuseum.org

Known locally as The Met, this museum is the largest art museum in the United States and has been in operation since 1872.

There are 17 curatorial departments and the permanent collection has over two million works from all over the world.

The Met is situated along Central Park, and the inside boasts massive glass walls into which natural light floods.

Additionally, there is a Roof Garden which exhibits art, has a café and bar, and some of the best views of Central Park and the skyline in Manhattan.

The temporary exhibitions at The Met are usually very well-done and should be looked into before going. As the place is enormous, it's best to enter with a plan as to not get lost.

# Dining

## Cilantro

 4-6 to 68th Street Hunter College  212-537-4040

 Mondays to Thursdays from 11:00am to 11:30pm; Fridays to Saturdays from 11:00am to 12:00am; Sundays from 11:00am to 11:00pm

 1321 First Avenue  www.cilantronyc.com

Cilantro is a Mexican restaurant with substantial outdoor seating, fresh entrée options, and a pleasant atmosphere. Standard dishes – Quesadillas, Salads, Soups, and meat-based entrees – are all made with fresh ingredients and at reasonable prices ($10 to $18). They make a great guacamole as a side or appetizer.

## Serendipity 3

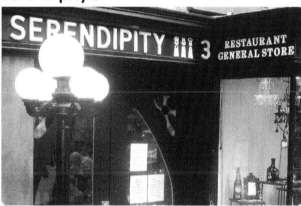

 N/Q/R to 59th Street Lexxington Ave

 212-838-3531

 serendipity3.com

 225 E 60th Street

 Sundays to Thursdays from 11:30am to 12:00am; Fridays to Saturdays from 11:30am to 1:00am

New York's first coffee house boutique, Serendipity 3 came into being in 1954. Since then, it's drawn celebrities, neighborhood residents, and visitors alike for it's rich delicacies.

While many go for the decadent entrees like Steak Char Char ($19) or the Bi-Sensual Burger ($19) many others also go for the unique coffee-inspired drinks. They're particularly famous for the Serendipitous Hot Chocolate ($6) and the Frrrozen Hot Chocolate ($9).

Serependity 3 also serves the world's most expensive sundae, the Golden Opulence Sundae for $1,000; the restaurant claims to sell one per month.

# Accommodation

## Carlyle Hotel

 6 to 77th Street

 35 E 76th Street

 212-744-1600

 www.rosewoodhotels.com/en/the-carlyle-new-york

This landmark hotel epitomizes luxury. Named after a Scotsman, Thomas Carlyle, the Art Deco styles provide an up-class environment for its guests.

It has 193 rooms and suites, many of which have beautiful views of Central Park. Amenities include a twice-daily maid service, 24-hour room service, complimentary delivery of major newspapers,

as well as access to a 24-hour fitness center. Rooms are some of the most expensive in the city, starting above $600. The even pricier options go for upwards of $15,000.

## The Franklin

 4/5/6 to 86th Street

 164 East 87th Street

 800-607-4009

 www.franklinhotel.com

An upscale option for a reasonable price is The Franklin Hotel. Rooms are priced between $300 and $400. The rooms here are not particularly spacious,

but they are indeed comfortable. It's often considered a romantic option, making it more suitable for couples. The following services are complimentary:

a European buffet breakfast, wine and artisanal cheese reception, and 24-hour espresso and cappuccino access.

## The Gracie Inn

 4/6 to 77th Street

 502 E 81st Street

 212-628-1700

 www.gracieinnhotel.com

This homey lodging option is in a house that was converted from a mansion to a boarding during the

Great Depression. Many decades later it was made into luxury apartments and now, the small inn provides a homey

atmosphere. There are 13 units, all with private bath. Room prices fluctuate between $200 and $300.

# Midtown

*Midtown is the idyllic place that most people visualize when they hear the words "New York City." Between Times Square, the Empire State Building, Rockefeller Center, and Broadway, this area is a tourist's mecca.*

During the day, the streets and sidewalks are overtaken by bodies in every direction. From people in the business, commercial, and financial sectors going between meetings, to tourists treading back and forth between museums, stores, and other sightseeing attractions.

In the evening, the neighborhood epitomizes one of NYC's main slogans, "The City That Never Sleeps." The nightlife comes out in full swing and the buildings light up in all their pride and glory. While many New Yorkers, due to their desensitization, will tell you that Midtown is over-rated and there is more of NYC to see, it's still an essential part of the NYC experience, and not to be over-looked.

# Attractions

## MoMA

 E/M to 53rd Street; B/D/ F/M to Rockefeller Center

 Adults: $25, Seniors (Over 65): $18, Students: $14, Children (Under 16): Free

 Saturdays to Thursdays from 10:30am to 5:00pm; Fridays from 10:30am to 8:00pm

 11 W 53rd St

 www.moma.org

The Museum of Modern Art (MoMA) is renowned for housing some of the most important modern art in the world.

Though it's been in operation since the early 1900s, renovations in 1983 and 2002 have doubled its original gallery size and made an open and modern structure.

The permanent collections are considered some of the best in world with famous artists such as Paul Cezanne, Marc Chagall, Salvador Dali, Frida Kahlo, Claude Monet, Henri Matisse, Andy Warhol, Pablo Picasso, Jackson Pollock, Vincent Van Goh, and countless others.

Temporary collections are usually regarded highly and appropriately timed.

Additionally, there are numerous Film exhibitions and events held throughout the year.

For those interested in contemporary art, the MoMA is an excellent place to spend the better half of a day.

# The Empire State Building

 N/Q/R/D/F to 34th Street – Herald Square     Daily from 8:00am to 2:00am

 Main Deck, Adults: $32, Seniors: $29, Children (6 to 12): $26, No wait: $55; Both Decks, Adults: $52, Seniors: $49, Children (6 to 12): $46, No wait: $75

 350 Fifth Avenue     www.esbnyc.com

If one skyscraper were to embody NYC, most people would agree it is the Empire State Building.

Since 1931, this 102-story building has enamored most of the world. For 40 years it stood as the world's tallest building but has since fallen in rank and is no longer even in the top 30.

The architectural design is representative of the Art Deco style and it has been designated a National Historic Landmark and one of the Seven Wonders of the Modern World.

Due to the building opening during the unfortunate time of the Great Depression, it took 20 years until it became profitable and inhabited.

Now, the Empire State Building houses 1,000 businesses and even has its own zip code.

The building can be visited, and the 86th floor observation deck is one of the most popular observatories in the world. For an additional fee, it is also possible to get to the 102nd floor. The lines tend to be long, and visitors can pay a fee to move to the front of the line.

# Times Square

 1/2/3/7/A/C/E/N/Q/
R/S to Times Square.     www.timessquarenyc.org

Times Square is a tourist's mecca; it is a commercial intersection that goes from West 42nd to West 47th Street and convenes at Broadway.

It is Times Square that has given NYC its reputation as the 'City of Lights' and it is certainly a sight to be seen.

At most times of the day, this intersection is flooded with people – many tourists as well as people in the business and entertainment industry.

The area is also known as the Theater District, as the surrounding streets house most of the Broadway musicals and plays. The TKTS booth at the northern end of Times Square is a good place to go for discounted theater tickets: sometimes they can be up to 50% off.

Times Square is home to Planet Hollywood, M&M's World, the Disney Store, and The Hard Rock Café.

We recommend experiencing Times Square during the nighttime to get the full effect of the lights and atmosphere.

# Bryant Park

 D/F/7 to Bryant Park  www.bryantpark.org

 January to Mid-March from 7:00am to 10:00pm; March from 7:00am to 8:00pm; April from 7:00am to 10:00pm; May from 7:00am to 11:00pm; June to September, Mondays to Fridays from 7:00am to 12:00am, Saturdays to Sundays from 7:00am to 11:00pm; October from 7:00am to 10:00pm; November to December from 7:00am to 10:00pm

 Fifth Avenue and W. 42nd Street

Bryant Park is a small park in the center of Manhattan. It's a serene place in the midst of skyscrapers and intensity.

Since 1686, the area, still considered the wilderness, was known as Bryant Park.

It was a graveyard for the poor until 1840, and most of the bodies were moved to present day Wards Island.

The New York Public Library joined the premises in 1899 and kiosks were added to the park.

During the 1970s the area was dangerous – a meeting place for gangs and drug dealers. However, in 1980, the Bryant Park Restoration Corporation sought to make the area safer and has since done a good job.

During warmer months, it serves as a common lunch spot for midtown workers. Kiosks serve sandwiches, salads, and other basic fare. Free Ping-Pong is available to play and there are a number of events held in the space, such as film screenings and free yoga classes in the summer. During the winter, an ice skating rink opens in the space as well.

# New York Public Library

 D/F/7 to Bryant Park      Free

 Mondays, Thursdays to Saturdays from 10:00am to 6:00pm; Tuesdays and Wednesdays from 10:00am to 8:00pm; Sundays from 1:00pm to 5:00pm

 Fifth Avenue and W. 42nd Street      www.nypl.org

The NYPL is a system with locations throughout the city; however, the main building is located at Bryant Park.

It is the largest public library system in the United States with 88 neighborhood branches and over 51 million items.

The combined public and private funding that the NYPL receives gives it innovative freedom and resources for many of its visitors to use.

Exhibitions and events are held annually at the library.

# Rockefeller Center

 B/D/F/M to 47-50th Streets; E/M to 50th Street

 Tour: $20; Combo: $42

 Daily from 7:00am to 12:00am

 45 Rockefeller Plaza

 www.rockefellercenter.com

This 22-acre complex housing 19 commercial buildings was declared a National Historic Landmark in 1987.

Its origins, beginning in 1930, made it the largest private building project ever undertaken at the time.

Used during WWII primarily for British Intelligence, the current center still houses the original Art Deco office buildings, as well as the Time-Life Building, McGraw-Hill, and Fox News headquarters, NBC studios, and various other renowned facilities.

Radio City Music Hall, a historic music hall famous for the presentation of the "Radio Christmas Music Spectacular," is an emblem of tradition in this area.

Other prominent features include the ice-skating rink plaza, open during winter months, and Diego Rivera's sculpture "Man at the Cross Roads" can also be visited on the premises.

Tours are given every half hour beginning at 10:00am and going until midnight (except 6:00pm to 7:00pm) and are priced at for $20/person.

It's also home to Top of the Rock (see the next page).

# Top of The Rock

 B/D/F/M to 47-50th Streets; E/M to 50th Street

 Observation deck, Adult: $30, Children (6 to 12): $24, Senior (Over 62): $28; Twice in one day Adults: $45 and Children: $36

 Daily from 8:00am to 12:00am

 30 Rockefeller Plaza

 www.topoftherocknyc.com

Although the Empire State Building has views of the city, the experience of going to the Top of Rockefeller Plaza offers, in our opinion, the best views of anywhere in the NYC area.

Upon entering, you'll go through a mezzanine exhibit detailing the story of Rockefeller Center and the Top of the Rock. Interactive components such as the beam walk put you in the shoes of the people who constructed the building.

After a short video, you'll enter the sky shuttle that will take you to the top.

At the top is an indoor space with comfortable seating and floor-to-ceiling windows where you can enjoy remarkable views.

An outdoor section, complete with binoculars, adds to the experience. Finally, a photographer is always on site to take photographs.

# St. Patrick's Cathedral

 E/M to 53rd Street     Free     Tours begin at 10:00am

 5th Avenue and 50th Street     www.saintpatrickscathedral.org

This neo-gothic cathedral church stands out in NYC among the skyscrapers and modern buildings.

The land under the cathedral was purchased in 1810 by a Jesuit community who then built a school. The cathedral was designed in 1858 but was not completed until 1878 due to Civil War delays.

The cathedral is the seat of the archbishop of the Roman Catholic Archdiocese of New York and it can accommodate up to 3,000 people. There are stained glass windows, roman sculptures, and various other pieces of artwork along the interior.

It's possible to just take a peek inside, or free tours are also offered.

# Grand Central Terminal

 4/5/6/S/7 to Grand Central 42nd Street

 Daily from 5:30am to 2:00am

 Audio tours - Adults: $9, Students, seniors, military and children: $7; Guided tours - Adults: $20, Students, seniors, military and children: $15

89 E 42nd Street

 www.grandcentralterminal.com

Although this is a regular commuter stop for many coming from Westchester and Connecticut, it's also an architectural and historical landmark.

With over 44 platforms today, it has more platforms than any railroad station in the world.

In 1871, the Grand Central Depot was opened to service the smaller railroads of the time. The original facilities were demolished at the turn of the century and two architectural firms teamed up to design the Beaux-Arts facility. Various institutions and businesses have cycled through Grand Central, including art galleries, stores, and restaurants.

The Main Concourse tends to draw the most tourists. In the center is a famous golden brass clock atop an information booth which serves as the most popular meeting place for people. The ceiling is a teal sky scape with constellations; it's entirely inaccurate, yet artistic nonetheless.

There are two ways to tour Grand Central. You can take a well-designed audio tour, which is available every day from 9:00am to 6:00pm. Alternatively, a guided tour is also possible, leaving every day at 12:30pm.

# Dining

## Ess-A-Bagel

 E to Lexington Avenue 53rd Street

 831 3rd Avenue

 Mondays to Fridays 6:00am to 9:00pm; Weekends 6:00am to 5:00pm

 212-980-1010

 ess-a-bagel.com

Many would contend that Ess-a-Bagel has the best bagels in the entire city. The original location was established in 1976 on 21st Street, but the midtown option provides the same options at the same quality. The owners came from Austrian families, where baking was a highly respected tradition.

The bagels are boiled to perfection, and there is a wide range of spreads to top them. Additionally, their pastries, muffins, cookies, and other treats will please a sweet tooth.

## Sushi Yasuda

 4/5/6/S/7 to Grand Central 42nd Street   212-972-1001

 Mondays to Fridays from 12:00am to 2:15pm, 6:00pm to 10:15pm, Saturdays from 6:00pm to 10:15pm

 204 E 43rd Street   www.sushiyasuda.com

Open since 1999, three founders – Naomichi Yasuda, Shige Akimoto, and Scott Rosenberg – have been successfully satisfying the sushi cravings of New Yorkers and visitors alike. The ingredients are local and the menu changes regularly, and it's likely that you'll spend over $100/person, but many report eating the best sushi they've ever had.

# Caffe Linda

 6 to 51st Street  646-497-1818

 Mondays to Friday from 11:30am to 11:00pm; Weekends from 5:00pm to 11:00pm

 145 E 49th Street  www.caffelinda.com

For a high-quality, simple, yet delicious meal, Caffe Linda is a solid option. Funny colloquial sayings are the titles for most of the options for the lunch menu. "Thumbs Up!" is a Grilled Chicken Caesar Salad ($14) or you can get a "Forget About It!" playing off of a stereotypical New Yorker phrase – a Mixed Grilled Vegetable Panini ($12). Dinner entrees have the Italian classics – various pastas, Chicken Milanese and Grilled Salmon ($16 to $20).

# The Halal Guys

 B/D/E to 7th Avenue; E/M to 53rd Street  N/A

 Sundays to Thursdays from 7:00pm to 4:00am; Fridays to Saturdays from 7:00pm to 5:00am

 53rd Street and 6th Avenue  www.53rdand6th.com

Halal food carts are a common fixture in NYC, but The Halal Guys have created a name for themselves that supersedes the rest.

They have numerous monikers under which they are known and serve the famous "Chicken & Rice" plate ($7).

They are open notoriously late and have served many drunken New Yorkers.

## Totto Ramen

 A/C/E to 50th Street   212-582-0052

 Mondays to Saturdays from 12:00pm to 4:30pm, 5:30pm to 12:00am; Sundays from 4:00pm to 11:00pm

 248 E 52nd Street   www.tottoramen.com

Although Ramen is traditionally a Japanese noodle soup dish, New Yorkers have fallen in love giving it a separate cuisine category in their city.

Totto Ramen is a popular spot for a reliable bowl. Naturally, they specialize in Ramen.

You can opt for a dish such as the Spicy Nibo – spicy fish, with scallions, bean sprouts, onion and cabbage ($13.50) or opt for the heartier Mega Ramen – with a variety of park, garlic, bean sprouts, and scallions ($15.50).

Customizable options are available as well.

## Bar Americain

 B/D/E to 7th Avenue; 1 to 50th Street   212-265-9700

 Mon 5:00pm to 10:00pm; Tues to Thurs 5:00pm to 11:00pm; Sat 11:30am to 2:30pm, 5:00pm to 10:00pm; Sun 11:30am to 2:30pm, 5:00pm to 11:30pm

 152 W 52nd Street   www.baramericain.com/nyc/

Celebrity chef Bobby Flay is the renowned chef behind Bar Americain – an American brasserie with bold flavors. Large appetizers like Spicy Tuna Tartare ($18) are great for sharing. Decadent entrees like Duck Confit with sweet and Sour Apricots ($38) and Gulf Shrimp & Grots with bacon green onions and garlic ($30) can be had, along with steaks and dishes of the day.

# Accommodation

## Waldorf Astoria

 6 to 51st Street; E/M to Lexington Avenue

 212-872-1275

 301 Park Avenue

 www.waldorfnewyork.com

Possibly the most historic hotel in New York is the Waldorf Astoria. The original facility was opened in 1893 on the site of William Waldorf Astor's Mansion on 5th Avenue and 33rd Street.

The second was opened at the current location in 1931 and catered to elite visitors.

Conrad Hilton took control in 1949 and in 1993 it became an official NYC landmark.

From the smaller guest rooms, to the enormous top floor towers, all the rooms meet high standards of luxury and are decorated with high-quality antiques. Rooms start at $300 to $500 per night.

## Pod 39

 4/5/6 to 42nd Street

 212-865-5700

 145 E 39th Street

 www.thepodhotel.com

An option on the cheaper side suitable to some younger travelers is Pod 39. A modern lodging option with a café, bar, and playroom onsite, provides small but comfortable rooms. They vary in size and amenities but most include Wi-Fi, safety features, and personal climate control. Rooms start at $150 to $200 per night.

## The St. Regis

 E/M to 5th Avenue 53rd Street

 212-753-4500

 2 East 55th Street

 www.stregisnewyork.com

One of the most expensive and luxurious hotels in NYC is the St. Regis. The hotel originally opened in 1904 by John Jacob Astor IV on 55th Street and 5th Avenue.

In 1960 it was bought by ITT Sheraton and after a remodeled 1991 renovation, the hotel is up and running.

While it's true to its origins of beaux-arts style, the renovations make it a place to feel like royalty.

With butler service top-level hospitality, you can rent rooms beginning at $600. They climb up to $1,000 or more depending on the style.

## Hotel Elysee

 E/M to 5th Avenue 53rd Street

 212-753-1066

 60 E 54th Street

 www.elyseehotel.com

In operation since the 1920s, Hotel Elysee has come to be known for its romantic and idyllic qualities. It was named for one of the finest French Restaurants of the decade that it opened.

Its classically beautiful architecture makes it a fine place to spend an evening. Included is a breakfast with pastries, fruits, eggs, and yogurt.

There are evening receptions each night from 5:00pm to 8:00pm serving wine, as well as a library of books and DVDs to enjoy. From single queen rooms to deluxe suites, prices range from $200 to $600 per night.

# Chelsea

*The name Chelsea was derived from the manor of Chelsea, London, home to English lawyer and philosopher, Thomas More. The area began to be developed in 1827. While Benjamin Moore sought to build well-designed residential buildings, industrial facilities began opening along the Hudson River.*

The increase in industrialization led to immigrants coming to Chelsea to work at the factories. Thus, tenements crammed with dwellers sparked riots and violence.

Theater, as a means of frustrated expression, came to the area and West 23rd street was originally the center of theater in the United States.

During World War II, a large amount of uranium for the Manhattan Project (atomic bomb) was stored in factories on 20th Street. The decontamination of the facilities did not take place until the 1990s.

Currently Chelsea is known for its artistic crowd as it is the epicenter of NYC galleries.

It is also known to have a large LGBT population and prides itself of upscale diversity.

Many of the old industrial factories have been converted into places to shop and entertain, adding to the gentrification of the area.

## Attractions

### Chelsea Market

| | | |
|---|---|---|
|  A/C/E/L to 14th Street | |  No admission charge |
|  Mondays to Saturdays from 7:00am to 9:00pm; Sundays from 8:00am to 8:00pm | | |
|  75 9th Avenue |  www.chelseamarket.com | |

In the former Nabisco factory complex lies Chelsea Market – a square block sized complex that has restaurants and shops that could occupy you for an entire day.

Events, such as pop-up shops, art shows, and concerts, occur throughout the year.

Food Tours are also available. These start at 10:00am, 10:30am, 4:00pm, and 6:00pm daily. They must be organized in advance but this is a great way to not miss the many tastes and the history behind the Market.

We think this is a must-do on any NYC itinerary.

# The High Line

 L at 14th Street; A/C/E at 14th or 34th; 1/2/3 at 14th or 34th Street

 Free

 December to March, daily from 7:00am to 7:00pm; April to May and October to November, daily from 7:00am to 10:00pm; June to September, daily from 7:00am to 11:00pm

 www.thehighline.org

The High Line is a new addition to NYC, opening in 2009, and has been immensely popular ever since.

This linear park was built on an elevated section of railroad called the West Side Line. It extends from Gansevoort Street to 34th Street and is best experienced from walking one end to the other.

It passes under Chelsea Market – a sizable food hall on 15th Street – where many visitors break for a meal, and over the various art galleries that Chelsea is famed for.

Unique to the High Line are the interesting plants and landscaping that grow over the old train tracks.

Additionally, temporary art installations change throughout the year.

# Galleries

 A/C/E to 23rd Street

 Free

 www.chelseagallerymap.com

In recent years, Chelsea has become a mecca for contemporary art galleries. They fill the streets between 18th and 28th and between the avenues of 10th and 11th. Some of the most notable and prominent galleries in the world have outposts here, such as Agora Gallery, ACA Galleries, David Swirner, Gagosian Gallery and others. All of them are free to enter and browse, and most are open between 10:00am and 6:00pm, however you should check the hours before going.

## Chelsea Piers

 A/C/E to 23rd Street        62 Chelsea Piers        www.chelseapiers.com

Though historically Chelsea Piers was a significant set of piers where major ships such as the RMS Lusitania and the RMS Titanic were due to land, its current use is for sport and recreation. The complex has a health club, day spa, and facilities for nearly every sport imaginable. It also houses Chelsea Brewing Company, the only micro-brewery in Manhattan. Hours and Prices vary depending on activity.

## Rubin Museum of Art

 F/M/A/C/E/L/1/2/3 to 14th Street        Adults: $15 / Students and seniors: $10 / Children (Under 12): Free

 Mondays and Thursdays 11:00am to 5:00pm; Wednesdays 11:00am to 9:00pm; Fridays 11:00am to 10:00pm; Weekends 11:00am to 6:00pm

 150 W 17th Street        www.rubinmuseum.org

The Rubin Museum of Art houses a collection of Himalayan and Tibetan art.

Opened in 2004, this relatively new museum has gained critical acclaim for advancing the study and interest in Himalayan arts. On and off-site educational activities have made this institution be respected for its commitment to cultural education.

# Dining
## Billy's Bakery

 A/C/E to 23rd Street; 1 to 23rd Street        212-647-9956

 Mondays to Thursdays 8:30am to 11:00pm; Fridays 8:30am to 12:00am; Saturdays 9:00am to 12:00am; Sundays 9:00am to 9:00pm

 184 9th Avenue        www.billysbakerynyc.com

This 1940s-style bakery began iwith two guys who met in business school and wanted to share their love of sweets with NYC. They make a wide range of cakes, pies, cupcakes, and cookies. They're particularly known for their incredibly decadent red velvet cake and have other standard bakery options as well. However, they don't shy away from more innovative options like the Banana Nutella Cupcake or the chocolate covered pretzel cheesecake.

## Murray's Bagels

 A/C/E to 23rd Street; 1/2 to 23rd Street  646-638-1335

 Mondays 7:00am to 8:30pm; Tuesdays to Wednesdays 7:00am to 9:00pm; Thursdays to Friday 7:00am to 10:00pm; Weekends 7:00am to 7:00pm

 242 8th Avenue  www.murraysbagelschelsea.com/Home.html

This famous NYC bagel shop is notorious for not toasting in addition to making great bagels. Their "no toast rule" derives from their belief that a perfectly fresh and delectable bagel doesn't need toasting.

A simple bagel with cream cheese will run you $2.75, while opting for their classic sandwich, The Traditional – a bagel with nova scotia salmon, cream cheese, beefsteak tomatoes, red onions and capers – will run you up to $10.50.

They also have signature sandwiches like The Rueben – hot corned beef, Swiss cheese, Russian dressing and sauerkraut ($10.50), as well as other classic NYC combinations.

## Blue Bottle Coffee

 A/C/E/L to 14th Street/8th Avenue  510-653-3394

 Weekdays from 7:00am to 7:00pm; Weekends from 8:00am to 7:00pm

 450 W 15th Street  https://bluebottlecoffee.com/cafes/chelsea

Though Blue Bottle Coffee is a national roasting company/coffee shop with numerous locations, the one in Chelsea stands out.

It is situated in the former loading dock of the Milk Building and has two floors.

Downstairs is the standard coffee shop (with fantastic seasonally roasted coffees) and upstairs they have cuppings and various other events.

Notable is their coffee siphon bar – a 1840s French coffee brewing technique done in a glass siphon over a fire.

# Bottino

 A/C/E to 23rd Street     212-206-6766

 Tuesdays to Saturdays from 12:00pm to 3:30pm, 6:00pm to 11:00pm; Mondays from 6:00pm to 11:00pm; Sundays 5:30pm to 9:30pm

 46 10th Avenue     www.bottinonyc.com

Open since 1996, this restaurant specializes specifically in the Italian cooking of Tuscany. The dinner menu features light fare for appetizers such as the Fennel and Baby Arugula Salad ($9) or Bruschetta al Pomodoro ($6) and offers heavier options for the entrees like the New York Strip Steak with Tuscan-Style Corona Beans ($28) or Pan-Seared Tuna ($22). Particularly notable is an extensive and well-chosen wine list that match the dishes perfectly.

# The Meatball Shop

 1/2 to 23rd Street     212-257-4363

 Sundays to Thursdays from 11:30am to 12:00am; Fridays to Saturdays from 11:30am to 2:00am

 200 9th Avenue     www.themeatballshop.com

The Meatball Shop is a trendy option for high quality food at a reasonable price.

While you can get a traditional Meatball Hero, the place prides itself on the balls themselves, and sells them "naked."

With a choice of beef, pork, chicken, or vegetarian, and a choice of sauce, you'll get 4 meatballs, cheese, and focaccia bread for $8. A range of sides is available to have with the balls or on their own, and sliders can also be made with the locally sourced ingredients.

# Accommodation

## Highline Hotel

 www.thehighlinehotel.com

 180 10th Avenue

 212-929-3888

 A/C/E to 23rd Street

The Highline Hotel has 60 rooms, but each feels handcrafted. With locally sourced furniture, complimentary lush robes, and complimentary Intelligentsia coffee, the hotel oozes comfort and calm.

Rooms range from 200 to 500 square feet, with views of the Highline, the back garden, or Chelsea's streets. Free Wi-Fi, as well as calls to anywhere in the world are included with the stay. Rooms range from $350 to $650 per night depending on dates and specs.

## Chelsea International Hostel

 www.chelseahostel.com

 251 W 20th Street

 212-647-0010

 A/C/E to 23rd Street

The premier budget option in NYC is Chelsea Hostel.

This place has no frills. It's your bare bones hostel, good for young people who don't anticipate spending much time in the room.

Rates are fixed and vary on size and time of year, but can be as low as $54/night, a deal difficult to beat in Manhattan. They also offer kitchen facilities, lobby internet access, and a free breakfast.

# Flatiron

*The Flatiron District is named after the iconic Flatiron Building. Before the 1980s, the area was known as the Toy District due to the Toy Center buildings in its location. Since then, it has become much more residential and houses photography offices and publishing companies.*

Aside from the Flatiron Building itself, there is the Met Life Tower, which was the tallest building until 1913 when the Woolworth Building downtown was completed.

The neighborhood boundaries are small but there is still a fair amount of exploring that can be done.

# Attractions

## Flatiron Building

 175 5th Avenue           N/R to 23rd Street

This architectural marvel is one of the most photographed buildings in the city. It is currently the headquarters of numerous established publishing companies.

It was designed by Daniel Burnham with Beaux-Arts styling. Since it's inception, visitors have come to stare at it in amazement.

## Madison Square Park

 N/R to 23rd Street     Free

 Daily from 6:00am to 12:00am

 11 Madison Avenue     www.madisonsquarepark.org

Just across the street from the Flatiron Building is Madison Square Park.

What was once a swampy hunting ground in the 1700s, an army arsenal in the early 1800s, and a farmhouse turned vacant lot until 1847, is now a gorgeous public park.

Various events and festivals are held here throughout the year, and it is also simply a place to enjoy a nice day.

It's also the birthplace of Shake Shack, a popular New York burger stop.

## Museum of Sex

 N/R to 28th Street   Adults: $17.50, Students: $15.25

 Sundays to Thursdays from 10:00am to 8:00pm; Fridays to Saturdays from 11:00am to 10:00pm

 233 5th Avenue   www.museumofsex.com

The Museum of Sex presents the history, evolution, and cultural constructions of human sexuality.

Founder Daniel Gluck opened up with an exhibit called *NYC Sex: How New York City Transformed Sex in*

*America* and since 2009 has expanded its scope and coverage at the current location.

# Dining

## 11 Madison Park

 N/R/6 to 23rd Street   212-889-0905

 Thursdays to Saturdays from 12:00pm to 1:00pm; Mondays to Sundays from 5:30pm to 10:00pm

 11 Madison Avenue   www.elevenmadisonpark.com

The inner workings of chef Daniel Humm and Restaurateur Will Guidara have made this restaurant one of the best and most highly regarded in all of NYC.

Given three stars by the Michelin Guide, and highly rated elsewhere, the multi-course tasting menu highlights the natural agricultural advantages and culinary traditions of New York.

For $225 per person, many report having the best meal of their lives. The fifteen course tasting menu changes regularly based on seasonality.

## Shake Shack

 Daily from 11:00am to 11:00pm   N/R/6 to 23rd Street

 Madison Square Park   www.shakeshack.com

Shake Shack began as a hot dog cart in Madison Square Park in 2001. The success it had led to the opening of a kiosk in the park, which remains there today.

While the chain has expanded nationally and internationally, it has a huge and dedicated following in NYC. People will stand in line in Madison Square Park for up to an hour.

The classic Shack Burger is made with 100% all-natural Angus beef ($5.29 for a single, $8.09 for a double). They also have a vegetarian option, the Shroom Burger – a fried Portobello mushroom filled with melted cheeses ($6.99).

Fries and dogs are available but they're known particularly for their Shakes, floats, and custards ($5-$7). The burgers here are simple, fresh and delicious.

## Eisenberg's Sandwich Shop

 N/R/6 to 23rd Street   212-675-5096

 Weekdays from 6:30am to 8:00pm; Saturdays from 9:00am to 6:00pm; Sundays from 9:00am to 5:00pm

 174 5th Avenue   www.eisenbergsnyc.com

With a slogan like "Raising New York's Cholesterol Since 1929" it's evident that you're going to find a place with a lot of character.

This old-style New York Deli is a narrow shop, with classic red bar stools to eat at the counter. Small two-person tables and chairs line the wall just a few feet behind the counter stools.

However, for what Eisenberg's may lack in comfort, it more than makes up for in quality.

For a grab and go breakfast option they have classic Egg Sandwiches ($4 to $5).

They're known for their classic simple options like Tuna Melts and Hot Corned Beef Sandwiches ($7.50 and $11).

Also, some say this is the best place to get a traditional Egg Cream – a drink of milk, soda water, and chocolate syrup ($2).

# Accommodation

## The Flatiron Hotel

 www.flatironhotel.com

 212 839-8000

 9 W 26th Street

 N/R to 28th Street

The 65 rooms at the Flatiron Hotel provide oversized windows and various views of the city.

The boutique luxury hotel has Jacuzzi bathtubs, Swiss rainfall showers, and oversized beds. On the roof is Toshi's Penthouse – a terrace where events can be held and Toshi's Living Room, a musical venue.

Rooms start around $200 and peak at about $600, but discounted rates are available for longer stays.

## The Evelyn

 www.theevelyn.com

 855-468-3501

 7 East 27th Street

 6 to 28th Street

This boutique option has residential type rooms in the Art Nouveau Style. The style is inspired by the late 19th and early 20th century culture, particularly the music. In addition to complimentary Wi-Fi, coffee and tea, and morning pastries, rooms are equipped with linens, bathrobes, and C.O. Bigelow soaps and moisturizers. Rooms tend to range between $200 and $400.

## The MAve Hotel

 www.themavehotel.com

 212-532-7373

 62 Madison Avenue

 6 to 28th Street

Situated next door to the well-known coffee shop, Birch Coffee, The MAve provides a comfortable modern accommodation option. With hard wood flooring, burgundy headboards, and H20 Aquatics bath products, comfort is well contained and supplied in the room walls.

Expect to pay about $400 per night.

# Gramercy Park

*Gramercy Park is often considered one of the most private and secluded neighborhoods in NYC. This is in part thanks to the private, fenced-in park after which it is named, as well as the exorbitant apartment prices.*

The current location was in the middle of a swamp, which in 1831 was developed into a residential area.

Due to zoning laws, the buildings in this area are required to be less than 20 stories. Most the buildings are only 3 to 4 stories high, making the residential area all the quieter and private.

Numerous famous people have lived here in the past. Although it's hardly a haven for tourist attractions, it does provide pleasant strolls.

## Attractions

### Gramercy Park

 Between 19th and 20th Street; Between Park Avenue and 3rd Avenue

 6 to 23rd Street

Gramercy Park is a fenced-in park, which only the residents of the original lots surrounding the park are allowed to hold.

In 2012, 383 keys were in circulation. In the past, the park used to be opened to the public for one day each year, in the beginning of May. However, due to the influx of visitors, they stopped the event in 2007.

Now, visitors can simply wander the perimeter and imagine an idyllic life inside.

## Theodore Roosevelt Birthplace

 6 to 23rd Street           Free

 Tuesdays to Saturdays from 9:00am to 5:00pm

 28 E 20th Street           www.nps.gov/thrb/index.htm

Theodore Roosevelt was the only United States president to be born in NYC.

The site is closed until late 2016 for restoration purposes, but normally there are Park Ranger guided tours on the hour.

The area is run by the National Park Service, a rarity in NYC.

## The Gramercy Theater

 N/R/6 to 23rd Street    http://venue.thegramercytheatre.com

 127 E 23rd Street

The Gramercy Theater opened in 1937 as a movie theater and did not start offering different forms of entertainment until 1998.

It then began showing off-Broadway theater productions but was shut down in 2004.

In 2007, Live Nation purchased the space and it has been turned into a music venue showing a wide range of musical styles.

## Vintage Shopping

Gramercy is home to one of the highest concentrations of high-end vintage shops. Walking back and forth on some of the streets, you'll come across a lot of used-items stores that have themes and are well curated. While the cheaper options like Salvation Army can be found, you'll also come across an array of more expensive vintage clothes.

# Dining

## Pete's Tavern

 N/Q/R/4/5/6/L to Union Square

 212-473-7676

 Daily from 11:00am to 2:30am

 129 East 18th Street

 www.petestavern.com

After opening in 1869, Pete's Tavern is the oldest continuously operating restaurant in NYC. The menu is Italian-American, with classic seafood, fried, and meat options. One can opt for a simple meat or cheese ravioli ($16.50) or have a Veal Scaloppini ($22.50) with a side of French fries or onion rings. While not all of the combinations prove to be the most sensible, it gives the establishment a unique and distinguished flare.

## Irving Farm Coffee Roasters

 N/Q/R/4/5/6/L to Union Square

 212-995-5252

 Weekdays from 7:00am to 10:00pm; Weekends from 8:00am to 10:00pm

 71 Irving Place

 www.irvingfarm.com

Whether you're just dropping in for a cup of coffee or staying for lunch, this little shop will please anyone's cravings.

From deliciously roasted coffee, to sweet pastries, to fresh salads and sandwiches, Irving Farm Coffee Roasters offers a delicious lunch or beverage option at this original location.

## Gramercy Tavern

 N/Q/R/4/5/6/L to Union Square

 212-477-0777

 Sundays to Thursdays from 12:00pm to 11:00pm; Fridays to Saturdays from 12:00pm to 12:00am

 42 E 20th Street

 www.gramercytavern.com

For a fine dining experience in the neighborhood, it's hard to beat the Gramercy Tavern. The restaurant serves locally-sourced meals throughout the year.

In the tavern, you can order a wide range of dishes a la carte. Sea Bass, Duck Leg, Lobster Broth – you name it, they prepare it to perfection.

The dining room offers both prix fixe options ($92) and tasting menus, both vegetarian and meat based ($102 and $120).

# Accommodation

## The Marcel at Gramercy

 www.themarcelatgramercy.com

 212-696-3800

 201 E 24th Street

 6 to 23rd Street

The Marcel offers 136 guestrooms, a 10th floor business lounge, and a rooftop terrace with complimentary wine tasting. Rooms are spacious, comfortable and usually fall within the $300 to $400 per night range.

# Ye Olde Carlton Arms Hotel

 www.carltonarms.com

 212-696-3800

 160 E 25th Street

 4/6 to 23rd Street

Since this building's construction over 100 years ago, it's primarily served as a hotel.

The name of this 54-room establishment plays off the history of the Irish presence in the area during the prohibition era.

A number of artists passed through the hotel in the 1970s and 1980s and the walls still hold some of their murals and fingerprints.

This budget option starts at $80 for one person and a shared bathroom, and goes up to $200 for four people with a private bath.

# Gramercy Park Hotel

 www.gramercyparkhotel.com

 212-920-3300

 2 Lexington Avenue

 6 to 23rd Street

All the furnishings, both large and small, have been hand-chosen and are highly valued at the Gramercy Park Hotel. Many of them come from famous artists, such as Julian Schnabel.

The rooms are composed of vibrant colors reflecting the renaissance revival style of the institution.

The hotel's walls are like a museum; works of Andy Warhol, Jean-Michel Basquiat, Keith Haring, and others, have working handing in the hallways.

Even the on-site dining is some of the best in the city, coming from Danny Meyer's renowned hospitality group.

Rooms begin just below $500/night and climb to over $1,000.

Guests of this hotel can sign out one of six keys to enter the exclusive Gramercy Park.

# Union Square

*Although Union Square Park is relatively small in geography, it is rich in action, history, and significance. Noted for an equestrian statue of George Washington and other statues, Union Square has become known for being an epicenter of social and political activism.*

Since 1861, Union Square became the site of rallies when it is said a quarter of a million people gathered to rally.

In the more recent years, the square has served similar purposes. After the 9/11 attacks, numerous people gathered to mourn in the city park.

It was also a central meeting point for the Occupy Wall Street movement. On any given day protesters and activists can be found on the stairs urging you to hear their cause.

# Attractions

## Union Square Greenmarket

 4/5/6/L to Union Square

 Free

Mondays, Wednesdays, Fridays, and Saturdays from 8:00am to 6:00pm

 Union Square Park

 www.grownyc.org/greenmarket/ manhattan-union-square-m

In 1976, the greenmarket began with just a few farmers in Union Square. They would sell products to a small number of

followers. The market has since grown into one of the most popular urban markets in the area.

People of all ages come to sample and purchase high-quality farmed goods in the middle of an urban metropolis.

## Irving Plaza

 4/5/6/L to Union Square

 Varies.

 Varies according to shows.

 17 Irving Place

 www.irvingplaza.com

This ballroom-style music venue can house over 1,000 patrons. From 1948 to 1976, the space was a Polish-American community center, but in 1978 it was converted into a rock music venue. Run by Live Nation, the venue showcases a wide range of contemporary musical artists.

# Dining

## Grey Dog

 N/Q/R/4/5/6/L to Union Square

 212-414-4739

 Sundays 7:30am to 10:30pm; Mondays 7:00am to 10:30pm; Tuesdays to Fridays 7:00am to 11:30pm; Saturdays 7:30am to 11:30pm

 90 University Place

 www.thegreydog.com

The Grey Dog is a reliable place to go with options for everyone. They don't serve up anything super fancy, but what they do make is just what you need. The challah French toast ($10) and Delaware Baked Oatmeal ($10) are favorites, along with the Breakfast Quesadilla ($12.50). For the rest of the day, they serve up sandwiches, salads, and combinations. Or, you can simply get a coffee, tea, or beer and no one will bother you.

# Nanoosh

 N/Q/R/4/5/6/L to Union Square

 212-397-0744

 Weekdays from 11:00am to 10:00pm; Weekends from 12:00pm to 10:00pm

 111 University Place

 www.nanoosh.com

This small NYC chain delivers Mediterranean food with fresh ingredients at reasonable prices. Soups, salads, wraps, and power food plates give vegetarians and vegans plenty to choose from, while also providing meat lovers with some solid options ($9 to $13). Almost everything is served with warm fresh-baked pita.

# Patsy's Pizza

 N/Q/R/4/5/6/L to Union Square

 212-533-3500

 Sundays to Thursdays from 11:30am to 11:00pm; Fridays to Saturdays from 11:30am to 12:00am

 67 University Place

 www.patsyspizzeria.us

Around since 1993, Patsy's has been serving reliably delicious thin crust pizza and other Italian food. Not sold in slices, the pizzas can be customized with toppings of various vegetables and ricotta cheese. Nearly everything on the menu is served family style, which are enormous portions to be shared by 4 to 5 people.

# 5 Napkin

 N/Q/R/4/5/6/L to Union Square

 212-228-5500

 Weekdays from 11:30am to 12:00am; Weekends from 11:00am to 12:00am

 150 E 14th Street

 www.5napkinburger.com

Although the original location was in Hells Kitchen, the location near Union Square is probably the best option for burgers. They offer a range of burgers from the '5 Napkin burger' which is 10 ounces of fresh ground beef, gruyere cheese, and caramelized onions atop a roll ($16.75). Other options are the Bacon cheddar, the Ahi Tuna, and the Veggie ($14 to $18). Also on the menu are Asian inspired foods like sushi, or teriyaki salmon bowls ($15).

## Max Brenner

 N/Q/R/4/5/6/L to Union Square

 646-467-8803

 Sundays to Thursdays from 9:00am to 12:00am; Fridays to Saturdays from 9:00am to 2:00am

 841 Broadway

 www.maxbrenner.com

To put it simply, Max Brenner is a place to indulge. The restaurant is all about serving up chocolate in new and different ways.

Beverages include the Chocolate Martini – with chocolate, Absolut vanilla, crème de cacao, and garnished with a strawberry ($13).

While they do have an extensive menu of standard sandwiches, salads, and other dishes, looking at the dessert menu is where imaginations really run wild.

Milkshakes like the Cookieshake – blended with Oreo cookies to the Peanut Butter

Turtle Choctail ($8) are available.

You can also opt for things like Dark Chocolate Covered Cherry Waffles ($14) or the popular Chocolate Chunks Pizza (half $9.50, whole $18). There are countless other options too.

# Accommodation

## W New York

 www.wnewyorkdowntown.com

 212-253-9119

 201 Park Avenue

 N/Q/R/4/5/6/L to Union Square

This modern urban lodging accommodation has rooms designed to be provocative and invoke sensuality. The hotel is pet friendly, has a fitness center, free Wi-Fi, and access to the restaurant terrace. While regular rooms can be reserved for just under $500, deluxe suites climb all the way up to $2,100.

## Hyatt Union Square

 www.unionsquare.hyatt.com/en/hotel/home.html

 134 4th Avenue

 212-253-1234

 N/Q/R/4/5/6/L to Union Square

This luxury option offers 178 rooms designed by established interior designer Paul Vega. His style combines high- technology designs with natural imagery. In a historic building with modern amenities, this is certainly a traditional combination of the old and the new. From studios to deluxe suites rooms progress from $400 to $2,000.

## The Inn at Irving Place

 www.innatirving.com

 56 Irving Place

 212-533-4600

 N/Q/R/4/5/6/L to Union Square

This is a private and somewhat elusive place to stay. There are no signs that are indicators of the location; simply the address is displayed. With 12 guest rooms, suites, and residences, the designers have taken care to furnish each room carefully with hand-selected antiques. Rooms range from $445 to $645 per night and include the basics. Situated on the lovely Irving Place this is a quiet, secluded, and quaint option.

## Hotel 17

 www.hotel17ny.com

 225 E 17th Street

 212-475-2845

 N/Q/R/4/5/6/L to Union Square

For a less expensive option than many of the others in the neighborhood, Hotel 17 offers a comfortable stay. It by no means has the same quaintness or design prowess as other options, but complimentary Wi-Fi, daily maid service, and a great location make for a pretty decent deal.

Rooms start at $120.

# Greenwich Village

*Greenwich Village has been referred to as the cultural capital of the world by some. Many call it just "the Village," which indicates a location of progressive, and sometimes edgy, perspectives.*

It's known to be the starting place of the Bohemian movement, an epicenter of LGBT acceptance, and the start of the counter culture movement of the 1960s.

While the neighborhood has greatly changed in the past few decades due to gentrification, the remnants of the past movements can still be seen and felt in the general area.

New York University, one of the country's largest private nonprofit institutions with over 53,000 students is in the heart of Greenwich Village, as are other smaller universities such as Yeshiva University, The New School, and The Cooper Union. The presence of all of which has contributed to rising rent and living costs.

## Attractions

### Grey Art Gallery

 N/R to 8th Street; 6 to Astor Place; A/B/C/D/E/F/M to West 4th Street

 Suggested $3

 Tuesdays, Thursdays to Fridays from 11:00am to 6:00pm; Wednesdays 11:00am to 8:00pm; Saturdays from 11:00am to 5:00pm

 100 Washington Square East.

 www.nyu.edu/greyart/

The Grey Art Gallery, NYU's fine arts museum is right next to Washington Square Park. The idea behind the exhibitions is to preserve, study, document, and display representations of human culture. There are exhibitions of all different mediums of artwork throughout the year.

### Margo Feiden Galleries

 N/R to 8th Street; 6 to Astor Place

 Free

 Mondays to Fridays from 10:00am to 6:00pm

 15 East 9th Street

 www.alhirschfeld.com/index2.html

The Margo Feiden Galleries house a collection of Al Hirschfeld's drawings, paintings, lithographs, and various other artworks. The work is found inside a Stanford White Townhouse in the Village and provides a comprehensive overview of 75 years of work.

# Washington Square Park

 A/B/C/D/E/F/M to West 4th Street

 Free

 Washington Square Park

 www.nycgovparks.org/parks/washington-square-park

In addition to Union Square Park, Washington Square Park has served as a meeting place for cultural activity and protest.

While nearly all of the buildings surrounding the park belong to NYU, making it NYU's makeshift campus, it attracts people from all walks of life.

The two main features of the park are the arch and the fountain. The Washington Square Arch was conceived in 1889 to celebrate the 100-year anniversary of George Washington first becoming president.

The result was a wooden arch built north of the park and its popularity led to architect Stanford White designing a permanent marble arch modeled off of Paris' Arc de Triomphe in 1892, which stands prominently in the park today.

The central fountain was renovated in 1934 to serve as a wading pool. As the temperatures become warmer the fountain fills with water and residents and tourists alike come and play in the water.

When the fountain is empty it serves as a venue for prominent street performers to come and showcase their acts in front of large crowds.

Whether it's a man playing a saxophone, a full jazz ensemble, or a circus act, street performers can almost always be found in areas of the park.

## Blue Note

 A/B/C/D/E/F/M to West 4th Street

 212-475-0049

 131 W 3rd Street

 www.bluenote.net/newyork/index.shtml

Blue Note is one of the most distinguished jazz clubs in New York City, and arguably the world. Some of the most famous artists like Chick Corea, Chris Botti, Liza Minelli, Tony Bennett, Stevie Wonder, and various others have performed there over the years. They offer music every evening at 8:00pm and 10:30pm. Cover charges vary, and food and drinks are served.

## Comedy Cellar

 A/B/C/D/E/F/M to West 4th Street

 212-254-3480

 117 Macdougal Street

 www.comedycellar.com

The Comedy Cellar is a high-end comedy club in NYC that began in 1982 by Bill Grundfest. Some regular performers include Colin Quinn, Jim Norton, Darrell Hammon, Louis C.K., Dave Chapelle, and countless others. There are numerous comedy shows held nightly and they vary in price based on performance and time.

# Dining

## Artichoke Basille's

 A/B/C/D/E/F/M to West 4th Street

 646-278-6100

 Sunday to Thursday from 11:00am to 4:00am, with a late closign at 5:00am on Friday and Saturday.

 111 Macdougal Street

 www.artichokepizza.com

Artichoke Basille's is particularly well-known for their Spinach artichoke slice, which at $4 seems like a hefty chunk of change.

However, one of these slices and you'll feel like you don't need another meal in days.

In general, their other options, including the second most popular Margarita, the anchovy pizza, or crab pizza, all provide a sizable slice that will leave your mouth watering.

## Peanut Butter & Co.

 A/B/C/D/E/F/M to West 4th Street

 212-677-3995

 Sundays to Thursdays from 11:00am to 9:00pm; Fridays to Saturdays from 11:00am to 10:00pm

 240 Sullivan Street

 www.ilovepeanutbutter.com

Peanut Butter & Co., known for selling jarred peanut butters, has its only store in New York. While most are twists

on the traditional PB&J, more creative options like the Might Maple Sandwich, with crispy bacon, or The Heat Is

On – with chilled grilled chicken and pineapple jam, couple with peanut butter to make it an interesting meal ($8).

# Mamoun's

 A/B/C/D/E/F/M to West 4th Street     212-674-8685

 Daily from 11:00am to 2:00am

 119 Macdougal Street     www.mamouns.com

For a cheap, quick, and grab and go option, it's hard to find one better than Mamoun's.

Years ago they became famous for their cheap falafel sandwiches, which are now $3.50. They have a very spicy sauce that can be had with any of the dishes.

Other classic Mediterranean options like tabbouleh, baba ganouj, are all available at reasonable prices.

## Lupa Osteria Romana

 A/B/C/D/E/F/M to West 4th Street     212-982-5089

 Sundays to Thursdays from 11:30am to 11:00pm; Fridays to Saturdays from 11:30am to 12:00 midnight

 170 Thompson Street     www.luparestaurant.com

Opened in 1999, Mario Batali, Joe Bastianich, Mark Ladner, Jason Denton, all have a share in this establishment. The food is traditionally Roman with some New York influences.

While it is by no means cheap, for the level of prestige that these chefs and restaurateurs have, the prices are pretty reasonable. On the more expensive end are things like

Lamb Scottadito with Gnoccho Alla Romana ($34) or Octopus with Swiss Chard and Potato ($26). However, a simple Spaghetti con Pomodoro can be had for a reasonable $14.

# Joe's Pizza

 A/B/C/D/E/F/M to West 4th Street

 212-366-1182

 Sundays to Thursdays from 10:00am to 4:00am; Fridays to Sundays from 10:00am to 5:00am

 7 Carmine Street

 www.joespizzanyc.com

Owner Joe Pozzouli, after which Joe's is named, was from Naples, Italy and began serving pizza to New Yorkers in 1975.

This place is nearly always listed as one of the best pizzas in New York, often in the world. Further, Joe's serves authentic pizza; nothing super cheap, no knock

offs or fancy add-ons. There are 3 options – plain cheese, fresh mozzarella or Sicilian square. Pies range from $20-$24 and slices go for about $3.

# Third Rail Coffee

 A/B/C/D/E/F/M to West 4th Street

 646-580-1240

 Mondays to Fridays from 7:00am to 8:00pm; Saturdays to Sundays from 8:00am to 8:00pm

 240 Sullivan Street

 www.thirdrailcoffee.com

Some of the best coffee can be found in Greenwich Village at Third Rail Coffee.

They now brew Counter Culture Coffee and rotate different guest coffees on a regular basis.

A small, but tasty selection of pastries and snacks are available on site.

# Accommodation

## Washington Square Hotel

 www.washingtonsquarehotel.com

 212-777-9515

 103 Waverly Place

 A/B/C/D/E/F/M to West 4th Street

The Washington Square Hotel has historically been a meeting place for writers, artists, and visitors. The 152 rooms have been modernized, but still have stylistic remnants of the past. Rooms have terry cloth bathrobes and granite-top vanity tables along with traditional amenities. Rooms typically range from $300 to $500.

## The Marlton Hotel

 www.marltonhotel.com

 212-321-0100

 5 W 8th Street

 A/B/C/D/E/F/M to West 4th Street

Even though The Marlton Hotel doesn't necessarily have the most spacious rooms, the architecture is certainly something to be admired. The rooms and other facilities have been tastefully designed. Rooms start at $350.

## Lafayette House

 www.washingtonsquarehotel.com

 212-505-8100

 38 E 4th Street

 A/B/C/D/E/F/M to West 4th Street

Situated in a 'brown stone' constructed in 1848, this lodging option offers rooms with antique furnishings and homey features like a fireplace. Staying here will give you the feeling of living in an upscale apartment and give you an idyllic vision of what it means to be a New Yorker. Rooms start at about $400 per night.

# West Village

*Although some do not distinguish between Greenwich Village and the West Village and group them together, in recent years the West Village has created an identity for itself separate from its surroundings.*

It earned the informal nickname "Little Bohemia" in 1916 and has been a constant source of housing for artists.

The neighborhood is entirely off of the Manhattan grid, and the streets are narrower and move in different formations than the rest of most of the city.

Due to the confusing geographic nature, this is an area seldom visited by tourists.

# Attractions

## Stonewall Inn

 1 to Christopher Street; A/B/C/D/E/F/M to West 4th Street

 Daily from 2:00pm to 4:00am

 53 Christopher Street

 www.thestonewallinnnyc.com

This bar in NYC was the site of the Stonewall riots of 1969 – violent demonstrations by the gay community. Consequently, it is known to be a founding place for the gay liberation movement.

Renovated and reopened in 1999 by the Greenwich Village Society for Historic Preservation, it's been declared a National Historic Landmark and has developed into hosting musical artists, drag shows, cabaret, and other types of entertainment.

## Westbeth Artists Community

 1 to Christopher Street           Free

 Wednesdays to Sundays from 12:00pm midday to 6:00pm

 55 Bethune Street           www.westbeth.org

This nonprofit housing complex was designed to offer living and working space for artists in NYC.

It was the site of Bell Laboratories from 1868-1966 and opened in 1970 for artists of various backgrounds.

Galleries and performance spaces are situated throughout the space and many notable and prominent artists have lived and worked there in the past.

## The Whitney

 A/C/E/L to 14th Street           Adults: $22, Students and seniors: $18, and Children (under 18): Free

 Mon 10:30am to 6:00pm; Wed 10:30am to 6:00pm; Thurs to Sat 10:30am to 10:00pm; Sun 10:30am to 6:00pm

 99 Gansevoort Street           www.whitney.org

Started by Gertrude Vanderbilt Whitney in 1931, The Whitney's collection is focused on exhibiting works of living and contemporary artists.

The original location was in the West Village but from 1966-2014 the location was in the Upper East Side. In 2015, they opened up a new main building, which is more expansive and open-plan than the old ones.

# Dining
## McNulty's Tea & Coffee

 1 to Christopher Street

 212-242-5351

 Mondays to Saturdays from 10:00am to 9:00pm; Sundays from 1:00pm to 7:00pm

 109 Christopher Street

 www.mcnultys.com

Many consider McNulty's a New York cultural institution. With over 100 kinds of loose-leaf tea, and old ceilings and walls, the odors that reach the sidewalk beckon visitors to see this establishment that has been around since 1895.

Whether you're planning on making a purchase or just browsing, this is an interesting and unique place to visit.

## Magnolia Bakery

 1 to Christopher Street

 212-462-2572

 Sundays to Thursdays from 9:00am to 11:30pm; Fridays from Sat 9:00am to 12:30am midnight

 401 Bleecker Street

 www.magnoliabakery.com

This famous bakery opened in 1996 at the Bleecker Street location in the West Village.

While it makes a range of desserts, it has become known for its irresistible rich cupcakes. They have a classic vanilla and chocolate, not to be overlooked, as well as specialty creative cupcakes like the Hummingbird – banana, pineapple, and pecan cake with cream cheese icing ($3.50).

Another popular choice is the banana bread pudding.

## The Cornelia Street Café

 A/B/C/D/E/F/M to West 4th Street

 212-989-9319

 Sundays to Thursdays from 10:00am to 12:00 Midnight; Fridays to Saturdays from 10:00am to 1:00am

 29 Cornelia Street

 www.corneliastreetcafe.com

The Cornelia Street Café doubles as a restaurant and a literary venue. Since 1922, the space has been devoted to presenting a variety of arts. People like Suzanne Vega and Oliver Sacks have performed and presented here, and there is normally more than one performance each night. The menu is upscale café food. Starters are available like a Locally Smoke Salmon Plate ($14) or a Strawberry, Walnut and Arugula salad ($12). More decadent options like the Magret of Long Island Duck ($25) or Sweet Corn and Mushroom Risotto ($18) are also on offer.

## One If By Land, Two If By Sea

 1 to Christopher Street

 212-255-8659

 Sundays to Thursdays from 5:30pm to 9:30pm; Fridays to Saturdays from 5:15pm to 11:15pm

 17 Barrow Street

 www.oneifbyland.com

At this fine dining establishment the A la Carte menu is only available at the bar. A prix fixe menu is $95 or you can do the tasting menu of 7 courses for $129. It is considered to be one the most romantic restaurants in all of NYC, serving dishes like spiced beef tartare with ginger, black plum, and bonito aioli and Maine Lobster bakes. The bold red walls and charming ambience make this a popular destination for marriage proposals and anniversaries.

# Accommodation

## The Jane

 www.thejanenyc.com

 212-924-6700

 113 Jane Street

 A/C/E/L to 14th Street

The Jane was built by the same architect that designed Ellis Island's immigration station. It began as the facility for the American Seaman's Friend Society Sailor's Home and Institute in 1908 and housed Titanic survivors in 1912 for a long period of time.

During the 1980s and the 1990s the hotel was a meeting place for people involved in the Bohemia movement.

Now, rooms have rainfall showerheads, marble sinks, and river views and terraces, while still keeping stylistic remnants of the past. Rooms are small and compact, starting at $115.

## The Standard, High Line

 www.standardhotels.com/high-line

 212-645-4646

 848 Washington Street

 A/C/E/L to 14th Street

This modern chain option has 338 rooms with floor-to-ceiling walls that allow you to marvel at the Hudson River. Comfortable beds are fitted with Italian sheets and extra large bath towels are provided to everyone. There is a 24-hour fitness center, a seasonal rooftop bar, complimentary bikes, and an ice skating rink in the winter. Rooms begin at $500/night and climb to $2,000.

# East Village

*Until the 1960s, the current space of the East Village was considered part of the Lower East Side. However, with an influx of students, musicians, artists, and hippies, it began to establish its own identity.*

Numerous and diverse artistic movements have originated in the East Village, including punk rock and the Nuyorican literary movement.

Eastern Europeans began flooding the neighborhood around 1850. German, Poles, and Ukranians created a strong community in the neighborhood. Although it has become incredibly gentrified in the past few decades, certain old family-owned eastern European institutions are still in place.

Arts and culture movements of the 1960s and 1970s hit a peak and began to decline as the 1980s rolled around. For a period of time the area was considered unclean and unsafe. However, the streets are now filled with a wealthier young crowd and is considered a fun and hip place to be.

## Attractions

### Nuyorican Poets Café

Since its founding in 1973 in a Rutgers University professor's apartment, this non-profit establishment has grown to be a cultural and literary haven. During big migrations of Puerto Ricans to NYC, there was a demand to establish a Puerto Rican/New York (Nuyorican) identity and place to speak freely.

The venue today has Open Mic nights, Poetry Slams, musical performances, and various other events.

 F to 2nd Avenue

 Mon 12:00pm to 12:00am; Tues to Frid midday to 2:00am; Sat 5:00pm to 2:00am; Sun 5:00pm to midnight.

 Varies by event.

 236 E 3rd Street

 nuyorican.org

# Tompkins Square Park

 L to 1st Avenue     $ Free     7:00am to dusk daily

 500 E 9th Street     www.nycgovparks.org/parks/tompkins-square-park

Situated in what's known as Alphabet City, this small square has turned from a high-crime, drug, and homeless area, to a place for East Village residents to spend an afternoon reading or talking over coffee.

A local playground and dog park make it an easy and comfortable place for residents to let their pets and children roam free.

The Tompkins Square Dog Run was the first one in NYC and the park is also noted for its stunning Elm trees.

A number of restaurants and delis line the border making it a great place to grab food and have a picnic.

# KGB Bar

 F to 2nd Avenue     Event hours vary. See website.

 85 E 4th Street     www.kgbbar.com

This Soviet-era themed bar used to be a speakeasy for Ukrainian Socialists who felt compelled to hide during the McCarthyism era.

Now, it's a dive bar/venue for literary readings. Events and readings are usually held nightly.

## The Ukrainian Museum in New York City

 6 to Astor Place

 Adults: $8, Students and seniors: $6, Children (Under 12): Free

 Wednesdays to Sundays from 11:30am to 5:00pm

 222 E 6th Street

 www.ukrainianmuseum.org/

Considered the largest museum in the United States dedicated to Ukrainian cultural Heritage, the institution has been supporting the local community since 1976.

The museum boasts an extensive folk art and fine arts collection, as well as an extensive archive of more than 30,000 items.

# Dining

## Box Kite

 6 to Astor Place; L to 1st Avenue

 212-574-8201

 Sundays to Mondays from 7:00am to 9:00pm; Tuesdays to Saturdays from 7:00am to 12:00am midnight

 11 St. Marks Place

 www.boxkitenyc.com

This new coffee shop serves far more than the average fare. The roasters and coffees served change on a regular basis according to what is in season, and what the barista is in the mood for.

Additionally, they've added a tasting menu for $85/person. Only 6 people fit at the bar and can experience the 8 to 10 course meal at a time.

The A la Carte options offer interesting options like a Fresh Chickpea Lasagna ($14) or a New York Strip Steak with Black Garlic Puree ($35).

## Abracao

 6 to Astor Place     N/A

 Tuesdays to Saturdays from 8:00am to 6:00pm; Sundays from 9:00am to 6:00pm. Closed Mondays.

 86 E 7th Street     www.abraconyc.com

In operation since 2007, this coffee shop is almost literally, a hole in the wall.

A tiny store front room for no more than 4 to 5 people draws visitors from all over the neighborhood on a regular basis.

It is consistently rated one of the best coffee shops in all of NYC, and for good reason.

There is also a small, but delicious collection of savory sweets. This place is especially well known for its olive oil cake.

## Xi'an's Famous Foods

 6 to Astor Place     212-786-2068

 Sundays to Thursdays from 12:00pm midday to 10:00pm; Fridays to Saturdays from 12:00pm midday to 11:00pm

 81 St. Mark's Place     www.xianfoods.com

This small NYC Chinese chain began in Flushing, Queens, in 2005.

They specialize in the regional cuisine in the area of Xi'an – a region that fuses Chinese and middle eastern flavors.

Menu options include Stewed Pork Hand-Ripped Noodles ($7) or Stewed Oxtail Hand-Ripped Noodles in Soup ($9), as well as the smaller options like a Spicy Cumin Lamb Burger ($3.50).

Prices for the authentic quality make it an absolute steal.

## Veniero's

 6 to Astor Place; L to 1st Avenue

 212-674-7070

 Sundays to Thursdays from 8:00am to 12:00am midnight; Fridays to Saturdays from 8:00am to 1:00am

 342 E 11th Street

 www.venierospastry.com

Veniero's was started by an Italian immigrant, Anthony Veniero, in 1894. By 1931, he had expanded his menu to a variety of cakes from biscotti, and passed on his family recipes after his death.

This is a New York historical institution, as well as a local favorite for desserts. They have over 200 pastry options to choose from, and few have said any are less than delicious. The cannoli, in particular, has a good reputation.

## McSorley's Old Ale House

 6 to Astor Place

 15 E 7th Street

 Mondays to Saturdays from 11:00am to 1:00am; Sundays from 1:00pm to 1:00am

McScorley's is the oldest "Irish" tavern in NYC. In operation since 1854, the pub only began letting women inside after 1970.

Old artwork and newspaper articles cover the walls, and the waiters and staff are what many consider "true Irish." Sawdust covers the floor and the inner décor makes you feel like you could be sitting alongside many of the famous patrons in the past like Abraham Lincoln or Teddy Roosevelt.

There is not a slew of options here; you either get a light or a dark ale, or more typically, one of each. Basic fare is also served.

## Momofoku Noodle bar

 6 to Astor Place; L to 1st Avenue

 212-777-7773

 Mon to Fri midday to 4:30pm; Sat & Sun midday to 4:00pm; Sun to Thurs 5:30pm to 11pm; Fri & Sat 5:30pm to 1:00am

 171 1st Avenue

 www.momofuku.com/new-york/noodle-bar/

This was the first Momofoku restaurant, and has now become a highly regarded institution. The menu changes according to ingredients and seasons but pork buns, ramen noodle bowls, and smaller snacks comprise most of the menu. They're also known for serving whole fried chicken in southern style and Korean style for reserved parties between 4 and 8 people. Snacks are $2 to $6, small dishes $9 to $16, and large dishes $12 to $18.

# Accommodation

## The Standard

 www.standardhotels.com/east-village

 212-475-5700

 25 Cooper Square

 6 to Astor Place

This modern chain option has 21 floors with 145 rooms with floor-to-ceiling windows that allow you to marvel at the East Village views. Comfortable beds are fitted with Italian sheets and extra large bath towels are provided to everyone. Guests can use the gym across the street at Crunch Bowery, and have access to daily newspapers. Rooms begin at $500/night and climb to $2,000.

## East Village Hotel

 www.eastvillagehotel.com

 646-429-9184

 147 1st Avenue

 6 to Astor Place; L to 1st Avenue

This lodging option makes you feel like you are staying less in a hotel and more in a walkup apartment in the neighborhood.

Studio style rooms are equipped with a Simmons Beautyrest pillow top bed and with full kitchens. Rooms fluctuate between $320-$360/night.

# The Bowery Hotel

 www.theboweryhotel.com

 212-505-9100

 335 Bowery

 6 to Bleecker Street

With 17 stories and 135 rooms and suites, all of the rooms follow a residential loft design with plenty of natural light and space. Rooms are adorned with hardwood floors and Oushak rugs, along with velvet drapes, 400 Thread Count Egyptian Cotton linens, and marble bathrooms.

Complimentary features include bicycles, a film library, New York Times newspapers, and WiFi. Pressing, Shoe Shine, Babysitting, and business services are available onsite. Room prices begin at $500/night.

# St. Marks Hotel

 www.stmarkshotel.net

 212-674-0100

 2 St. Marks Place

 6 to Astor Place

The go-to budget option in the area is The St. Marks Hotel. Prices for full sized bedrooms start at $93/night and go up to $145 for suites. If you are looking for a place right in the middle of the action, this is it. St. Marks is one of the liveliest streets in the neighborhood and you are a five-minute walk from nearly everything in the East Village.

# SoHo/NoLita

*The name SoHo came from the reference to its area "South of Houston Street" as well as in reference to London's Soho, an area known for arts. NoLita is a newly termed area, short for "North of Little Italy."*

Unique to the neighborhood is the cast-iron architecture, the biggest collection in the world. These unique industrial style buildings were primarily built from 1840 to 1880 with a rise in industrialization.

With growth of the artist population, and a decline in real estate prices, numerous artists moved to SoHo. The industrial lofts with massive windows were an appealing feature for those looking to have studio space in their homes.

As zoning laws changed in 1980s and the neighborhood began to fill with more affluent residents, many artists moved to the boroughs, and the galleries moved to Chelsea.

Currently, SoHo is known for its endless shopping opportunities. Boutique stores line the narrower streets, as do national and international chains.

Similarly, quaint cafes and bars along paved Belgian blocks make the streets a quaint place to wander around.

# Attractions

## Leslie-Lohman Museum of Gay and Lesbian Art

 1/2/A/C/E to Canal Street    Free

 Tuesdays to Sundays from 12:00pm midday to 6:00pm; Thursdays from 12:00pm midday to 8:00pm

 26 Wooster Street    www.leslielohman.org

This is the first dedicated LGBTQ art museum in the world. The permanent collection has over 24,000 works of (and about) LGBTQ artists, and showcases various exhibitions throughout the year.

## Shopping

SoHo has nearly every store, type, style, etc. available. Roaming the streets and going in and out of stores can provide for entertainment for those interested or curious in fashion. Whether or not you buy anything, it is worth a solid walk. Some interesting boutiques to check out are Babel Fair, Birchbox, COS, Evolution, Kirna Zabete, and others.

## New York City Fire Museum

 C/E to Spring Street

 Adults: $8, Students and seniors: $5, Children (Under 12): Free

 Daily from 10:00am to 5:00pm

 278 Spring Street

 www.nycfiremuseum.org

The original New York City Fire Museum opened in Long Island City, Queens in 1934. In 1959 the collection moved to Duane Street in Manhattan. The non-profit, The Friends of the New York City Fire Department Collection, helped move the collection to the place it is today – a renovated former firehouse built in 1904. This museum takes visitors through the history and evolution of the FDNY. There is a special memorial to the 343 FDNY members who lost their lives contributing to rescue missions after 9/11.

# Dining
## Blue Ribbon Sushi

 6 to Spring Street; N/R to Prince Street

 212-343-0404

 Daily from 12:00pm to 12:00am

 119 Sullivan Street

 www.blueribbonrestaurants.com

Often considered NYC's best sushi bar, Blue Ribbon Sushi is run by Toshi Ueki. Specials change daily and ingredients are flown in daily from the Pacific Ocean and Sea of Japan. Rolls go from $6 to $19 and specialty pieces are generally between $4 and $5. Numerous platter options are available and good for sharing.

## Café Gitane

 N/R to Prince Street  212-334-9552

 Sundays to Thursdays from 8:30am to 12:00am midnight; Fridays to Saturdays from 8:30am to 12:30am

 242 Mott Street  www.cafegitanenyc.com

This quaint Moroccan-style café serves healthy fare and three meals daily. They've made a name for a simple dish – Avocado on seven-grain toast ($7.25) and they serve other similar combinations atop fresh breads.

Salads and specials like Moroccan couscous provide excellent vegetarian options ($14) and mead can always be added for an extra $3.

## Balthazar Bakery

 6 to Spring Street; N/R to Prince Street  212-965-1785

 Mon to Fri 7:30am to 11:30pm; Sat & Sun 8:00am to 4:00pm; Mon to Fri midday to 5:00am; Mon to Thurs 6:00pm to midnight; Fri to Sat 6:00pm to 1:00am; Sun from 5:30pm to midnight

 80 Spring Street  www.balthazar.com

While you're likely to find their baguettes and other baked items sold throughout all of NYC, Balthazar also operates a restaurant in the SoHo location.

The French bakery serves classic bistro fare for all three meals of the day.

Decadent breakfast options include Eggs Benedict ($22) while simply getting a Fresh Florida Grapefruit is available as well ($10).

For lunch or dinner, bistro fare like Sautéed Skate with fava beans, radish, almonds, and onion ($31) can be had, as well as grilled Lamb T-Bones ($42).

However, if that is out of your price range, picking up some bread or a pastry will help provide you a taste worthwhile.

## Balaboosta

 N/R to Prince Street     212-966-7366

 Tues to Fri 11:30am to 3:30am; Sat & Sun 11:00am to 3:30am; Mon to Thur 5:30pm to 10:30pm; Fri & Sat 5:30pm to 1:00am; Sun 5:30pm to 10:00pm

 214 Mulberry Street     www.balaboostanyc.com

The name Balaboosta derives from a Yiddish term referring to the perfect housewife.

The menu is a new and fresh look at Middle Eastern and Jewish classics prepared with fresh ingredients and care.

Prix Fixe Menus are available for large parties and a lot of sharing is typical.

Starters like Crispy Cauliflower ($11) and Smoke Eggplant Bruschetta ($15) are simply but delectable.

The entrees are varied, from a Wild Red Snapper ($32) to Grilled Lamb Chops ($34) to the boneless Chicken "Under a Brick" with Israeli couscous, apricots, leeks, and gremolata ($27).

## Alidoro

 C/E to Spring Street     212-334-5179

 Mondays to Fridays from 11:30am to 4:30am

 105 Sullivan Street     www.alidoronyc.com/locations-1/

Alidoro makes one thing. And they make it really, really well: sandwiches.

It was founded in 1986 in the SoHo location and they pride themselves on simple but fresh ingredients; they don't Americanize, it's pure

Italian.

The ingredients are bought fresh from local sources except the meat, which is imported from abroad.

The sandwiches are big and hearty, but can certainly be shared.

Most are some combination of prosciutto, mozzarella, roasted peppers, arugula, chicken breast, and eggplant ($9 to $12). Cash only.

# Accommodation

## The Bowery House

 www.theboweryhouse.com

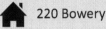 220 Bowery

212-837-2373

6 to Spring Street; J/Z to Bowery

This loft-style budget option originally opened as The Prince Hotel in 1927. After World War II it was used to lodge soldiers returning home from war. Bathrooms were communal and bedrooms made small. The hotel is dedicated to preserving that time period, albeit amid cleaner conditions.

Rooms, or cabins as they like to call them, are about $100/night.

## Crosby Street Hotel

 www.firmdalehotels.com/hotels/new-york/crosby-street-hotel/

 79 Crosby Street

 212-226-6400

 6 to Spring Street; N/R to Prince Street

Crosby Street is one of the quaintest streets in NYC. Nestled in a bustling area, the cobblestones and unique boutiques that line the sidewalks make it an idyllic place to take a brief relaxing stroll.

The hotel has 86 rooms with floor-to-ceiling windows letting in light and allowing for beautiful views of the city. Rooms are all upwards of $1,000.

## The Nolitan Hotel

 www.nolitanhotel.com

 30 Kenmare Street

 212-925-2555

 J/Z to Bowery

The Nolitan Hotel is described as boutique luxury. The 57 rooms are equipped with plush mattresses and lightweight comforters. A fitness center on-site offers free classes as well as free bikes and skateboards for guests.

A French restaurant is on-site serving three meals each day.

Rooms average $400/night.

# Lower East Side

*The Lower East Side (LES) is an old neighborhood oozing with a rich tradition and history*

Since immigrants began arriving in New York, the Lower East Side was where people of all different backgrounds – Irish, Italians, Poles, Ukrainians, Germans, and Jews – began forming cultural enclaves and communities.

Gentrification has certainly hit this neighborhood and it has changed.

More Dominicans and Puerto Ricans have moved in, as well as younger upper class adults. However, many of the older rent-stabilized institutions and family businesses have remained in tact.

It's a mixture of the old and new, but one of the few places in NYC where you can really get a sense of what it may have been like years ago.

## Attractions

### ABC No Rio

 F/J/M/Z to Delancey/Essex Street  www.abcnorio.org

 156 Rivington Street

Founded in 1980, ABC Rio is a collectively run art and activism center.

It has a gallery space, a darkroom, a zine library, a silk-screening studio and a public computer lab.

It is particularly well known for its Punk/Hardcore Collective, which hosts weekly matinees on Saturday afternoon.

# Tenement Museum

 J/Z to Bowery

 Adults: $25, Students and seniors: $20

 At set times. See website.

 www.tenement.org

 103 Orchard Street

The Tenement Museum is an unassuming institution on the Lower East Side that successfully brings the history of immigrants living in NYC between 1869 and 1935 to life.

For those interested in history, this is a prime spot to go, and for those not so interested, this is the place that may spark your curiosity.

The museum is only seen through guided tours. While initially it may seem unappealing to some, the staff is incredibly well versed, patient, and engaging.

They offer a few different kinds of tours that detail certain aspects of immigrant life, give waking tours of the neighborhood, and have actors that act as the residents of the tenement on Orchard Street. The tours go through recreated tenements and shops that accurately recreate the style of the time.

Additionally, the museum has a free bookshop with an interesting collection of books about or based in NYC, and various other NYC related trinkets.

Available with reservation only.

## New Museum

 F to 2nd Avenue; J/Z to Bowery; 6 to Spring Street

 Adults: $16, Seniors: $14, Students: $10, Children (18 and Under): Free;

 Tuesdays to Wednesdays from 11:00am to 6:00pm; Thursdays from 11:00am to 9:00pm; Fridays to Sundays from 11:00am to 6:00pm

 235 Bowery

 www.newmuseum.org

The New Museum was an idea conceived of by Marcia Tucker, who had been working at the Whitney Museum until 1976.

Having been frustrated with the lack of acceptance of artwork by living artists into museums, she set off to start her own.

When she officially founded the institution in 1977, it was the first museum devoted to contemporary art in NYC since World War II.

The seven story, eight-level structure of the building was designed by Japanese architects and is representative of the innovations of the inside work itself.

Thursday evenings from 7:00pm to 9:00pm are 'pay what you wish'.

## Bowery Ballroom

 B/D to Grand Street; F/J/M/Z to Essex/Delancey Street

 6 Delancey Street

 www.boweryballroom.com

This music venue in downtown Manhattan was a high-end retail store from the end of World War II until 1998. Now it serves as a music venue for a variety of artists with a capacity of 575 people. Check the website for show and event postings.

# Dining
## Katz's Delicatessen

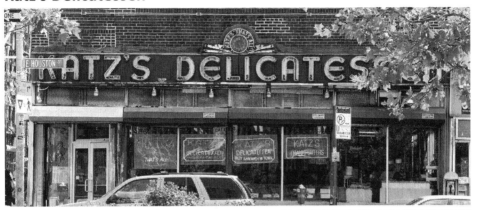

 F to 2nd Avenue     212-254-2246

 Mondays to Wednesdays from 8:00pm to 10:30pm; Thursdays from 8:00pm to 2:30am; Fridays to Saturdays from 8:00pm to 5:30am; Sundays from 6:00pm to 10:30pm

 205 E Houston Street     www.katzsdelicatessen.com

Few restaurants can fully capture the quintessential nature of NYC history like Katz's Delicatessen does.

Both tourists and locals frequent this kosher style deli, and it's particularly well known for the iconic sandwich, Pastrami on Rye.

Although the sandwiches may run you up to $17 or $18, they're massive and can be shared.

This is where Meg Ryan filmed the famous scene in 'When Harry Met Sally.'

Originally called Iceland Brothers, the first deli opened in 1888 by two brothers. Willy Katz joined the team in 1903, and Willy's cousin came to help buy out the Iceland brothers in 1910. Finally, in 1917, they moved across the street to the location today.

Always a neighborhood staple, during World War II the owners allowed people to send their sons salami with the slogan, "Send A Salami To Your Boy In The Army."

The deli still uses the old ticket system, where a door attendant hands a printed number ticket to keep track of the tab (a lost ticket fee is $50).

Coming to Katz's is like going to a museum and a restaurant at the same time.

## Russ and Daughters

 F to 2nd Avenue     212-475-4880

 Mondays to Fridays from 8:00am to 8:00pm; Saturdays from 8:00am to 7:00pm; Sundays from 8:00am to 5:30pm

 179 E Houston Street     www.russanddaughters.com

Another long-standing LES classic is Russ & Daughters. Open since 1914, the storefront remains the same as does the family-style atmosphere.

Joel Russ, a Polish immigrant, grew from selling Polish mushrooms from a Pushcart to selling pickled herrings from this new storefront.

Today, they serve the highest quality fish and caviar in the city. They make good bagels and the go-to combo is a traditional Bagel with Lox and cream cheese.

## Sons of Essex

 J/M/Z to Essex Street; F to Delancey Street     212-674-7100

 Tuesdays to Wednesdays from 6:00pm to 10:00pm; Thursdays from 6:00pm to 12:00am midnight; Fridays from 6:00pm to 4:00am; Saturdays from 11:00am to 4:00am; Sun 11:00am to 6:00pm

 133 Essex Street     www.sonsofessexnyc.com

This restaurant, though emblematic of gentrification, does so by calling on the roots of the past. The menu embodies American comfort food with new

age innovations, while creating an atmosphere of Old School Lower East Side in the restaurant.

Fresh salads ($15) and small plates like Truffle

Mushroom Pizza ($18) and Lobster Tostadas ($19) are great for sharing, while entrees include items like Lamb Skewers ($28) and Braised Short Ribs ($29).

## Mission Chinese Food

 F to East Broadway

 www.missionchinesefood.com

 Tuesdays to Sundays from 5:30pm to 12:00am midnight

 171 E Broadway

In 2013, chef Danny Bowien's Sichuan restaurant on the Lower East Side was closed by the health department. It was a devastating blow but he bounced back just a year later back in the Lower East Side and is doing better than ever. The new location, cleaner and more upscale, has 130 seats.

Patrons can order a la carte, or order a varying spread of Chinese delicacies ($69 to $99). Some of the menu options are less typical than you normally see in Chinese restaurant, and have influences of traditional American cuisine, like the beef jerky fried rice.

# Accommodation

## Hotel on Rivington

 www.hotelonrivington.com

 212-475-2600

 107 Rivington Street

 J/M/Z to Essex Street; F to Delancey Street

Rooms at this LES hotel are spacious, beginning at about 400 square feet each. Many rooms have balconies, soaking tubs, steam showers, and massive glass walls allowing light to flood in. Beds have Tempur-Pedic mattresses, soft linens, and high-end bath amenities. Rooms average about $400.

## Blue Moon Hotel

 www.bluemoon-nyc.com

 212-533-9080

 100 Orchard Street

 J/M/Z to Essex Street; F to Delancey Street

This boutique hotel is in a 19th century tenement building that has been converted to suit modern comforts, while maintaining some of the old features – wood moldings, old doors and light fixtures, and marble tiles. There are 22 rooms named after famous icons from the 1920s and 1930s. It has won a number of travel awards, including National Geographic's Best Boutique Hotel. Prices from $280.

# Tribeca

*While most people know it for the film festival, Tribeca (Triangle Below Canal Street) earned its own neighborhood name in the 1970s.*

As the neighborhood struggled significantly following the September 11 attacks, the Tribeca Film Festival was created to promote the recovery.

It has become, in recent years, a very upscale and desirable place to live.

Numerous celebrities reside in Tribeca, and it is often regarded as the safest neighborhood in NYC.

## Attractions

### Tribeca Cinemas

 www.tribecacinemas.com

 212-941-2001

 54 Varick Street

 1/A/C/E to Canal Street

In operation since 2003, this cinema has become a premier special event venue in NYC. There are two private screening rooms and The Varick Room – an event space that can accommodate larger events.

### The Mysterious Bookshop

 www.mysteriousbookshop.com

 212-587-1011

 58 Warren Street

 1/2/3 to Chambers Street

This is a bookstore unlike any other. They have a wide selection specializing in mystery novels and periodicals as well as other rare books. The environment and décor make this an enjoyable place to walk around, even if you don't plan on purchasing anything.

## The Flea Theater

 www.theflea.org

 41 White Street

 212-226-0051

 N/R to Canal Street;
1 to Franklin Street

Around since 1996, the Flea Theater was created by three theater artists seeking to create "a joyful hell in a small space." They host and promote off-off Broadway performances, many of which are innovative and experimental. Check the website and calendar for the upcoming productions.

# Dining

## Bouley

 1/2/3 to Chambers Street

 212-964-2525

 Mondays to Saturdays from 11:30am to 5:00pm, 5:00pm to 11:30pm

 163 Duane Street

 www.davidbouley.com/bouley-main/

Chef David Bouley's philosophy is to provide the freshest ingredients in innovative ways as they come into season.

The prix fixe menu at Bouley offers three courses, with options like a Wild Oregon mastutake mushroom, New York State Foie Gras, Organic Long Island Duck, Organic Colorado Lamb, New Zealand White Fallow Venison.

In short, you'll always know where your food is coming from. And it is always fresh.

The prix fixe menu is $125 with an option for an $85 Sommelier's wine pairing. The 6-course tasting menu goes for $185.

## The Odeon

 1/2/3 to Chambers Street

 212-233-0507

 Mon 8:00am to 11:00pm; Tues to Fri 8:00am to midnight; Sat 10:00am to midnight; Sun 10:00am to 11:00pm

 145 W Broadway

 www.theodeonrestaurant.com

This classic NYC joint has been around since the 1980s and serves top-quality bistro cuisine in a relaxed environment.

Serving three meals a day, the menu remains simple.

For breakfast you may opt for French toast with berries ($15), for lunch a BLT Sandwich on challah ($18) and for dinner a NY Strip Steak with Fries ($40) or Moules Frites ($24).

## Sarabeth's

 1/2 to Franklin Street

 212-966-0421

 Mondays to Fridays from 8:00am to 10:30pm; Saturdays from 8:00am to 11:00pm; Sundays from 8:00am to 10:00pm

 339 Greenwich Street

 www.sarabethsrestaurants.com

The Sarabeth's location in Tribeca is famous for their weekend brunch, but the other meal options are solid as well. They have a few other locations throughout the city and provide high-quality and reliable fare. For brunch they serve a few different freshly squeezed juices ($7) alongside super-sweet options like Lemon and Ricotta Pancakes or Coconut Waffles ($17) or famous omelets like Salmon Eggs Benedict ($19) which come alongside a pastry.

## Tiny's

 1/2/3 to Chambers Street

 212-374-1135

 Mondays to Thursdays 11:30am to 11:00pm; Fridays 11:30am to 1:00am; Saturdays 10:30am to 1:00am; Sundays 10:30am to 11:00pm

 135 West Broadway

 www.tinysnyc.com

The building in which Tiny's is located is from 1810, and some of the antiques are over 100 years old. Original tin ceilings, wood paneling, and antique wallpaper make the aesthetic of the place a nice place to enjoy a meal. Starters include items like the Salmon and Beet Salad ($14) or House Made Meatballs ($14). Entrees include the Castle Mill Valley Risotto" ($23) as well as a range of freshly prepared meats and fish ($25 to $35).

## Brandy Library

 1/2 to Franklin Street

 212-226-5545

 Sundays to Wednesdays from 5:00pm to 1:00am; Thursdays from 4:00pm to 2:00am; Fridays to Saturdays from 4:00pm to 4:00am

 25 N Moore Street

 www.brandylibrary.com

If you are into spirits, this is a good place to go. Although they've extended the indoor drinking age to 25 to provide a certain level of maturity in the dimly lit space, they provide rare alcohol, wines, and beers, as well as spirit classes. They also offer some food options – sandwiches, sushi rolls, and some sides. Whether you're coming for a pre- or post-meal drink, or are here to spend the whole night, this is a nice option.

# Accommodation

## Tribeca Blu Hotel

 www.tribecabluhotel.com

 212-941-6106

 276 Canal Street

 N/R to Canal Street

Situated in a cast-iron nine-story building, rooms are affixed with modern comforts and appliances. The rooms are nothing fancy, but for prices that begin at $170 per night, it's a solid deal in such a desired neighborhood.

## Tribeca Grand Hotel

 www.tribecagrand.com

 212-519-6600

 2 Avenue of the Americas

 1/2 to Franklin Street

This luxury option offers 201 guest rooms with high-end fixtures. Included are Egyptian cotton bed and bath linen, Frette bathrobes, and Malin and Goetz bath amenities.

Experienced hotel owners running the Soho Grand Hotel opened the Tribeca location in 2000, and rapidly experienced high acclaim. Rooms start at $450 per night.

## Cosmopolitan Hotel

 www.cosmohotel.com

 212-566-1900

 95 W Broadway

 1/2/3 to Chambers Street

The Cosmopolitan Hotel is one of the longest running hotels in NYC. Constructed in 1838 in a Gothic Revival style, the hotel expanded and was named the Cosmopolitan Hotel in 1869.

It has served some of the most prominent judges, lawyers, and politicians in the past, and continues to do so today. This boutique hotel offers a range of room types with high-end linens and both products. Rooms start at $380.

# Chinatown

*Most cities have a Chinatown of some kind, but Manhattan's Chinatown is home to one of the most densely populated areas in the West, with between 90,000 and 100,000 people.*

Chinese immigrants were restricted to migrating to only East Coast cities due to racial discrimination acts of the late 1800s, which is why the area became so highly populated.

When immigration reforms took effect in 1965, a massive influx of Chinese immigrants, specifically from Hong Kong, began coming to New York. Different languages, loyalties, and cultures, led to animosity between some groups. Chinese gangs began forming throughout the Lower East Side and gang warfare was present until the 1990s.

The population continuously moves to other areas of NYC and changes, but the unique grocery stores, restaurants, knock-off brands, and jewelry stores are still prominent in the area.

Many New York natives go there for authentic Chinese fare, or just to experience the busy and intense way of life.

# Attractions

## Museum of Chinese in America

Since 1980 this museum has been a hub to learn about, preserve, and present information on the history and culture of China. With various displays of history – from multimedia, to oral, to artifact presentation, the curators hope to cultivate a stronger understanding of Chinese-American history.

Free admission for all on the first Thursday of the month.

N/Q to Canal Street

Tuesdays, Wednesdays, Fridays, Saturdays, Sundays from 11:00am to 6:00pm; Thursdays from 11:00am to 9:00pm

215 Centre Street

Adults: $10, Students & seniors: $5, Under 12s: Free

mocanyc.org

# Dining

## Fried Dumpling

 4/6/J/Z to Canal Street   212-693-1060

 Daily from 10:00am to 9:00pm

 106 Mosco Street   www.frieddumplingnyc.com

Often considered the best dumplings in Chinatown and even more frequently dubbed the best overall value, this is a great option for an almost unbelievably cheap meal. Its usually $1 for 4 dumplings, and other items are very affordably priced too.

## Vanessa's Dumplings

 J/M/Z to Essex Street   212-625-8008

 Mondays to Saturdays from 10:30am to 10:00pm

 118 Eldrige Street   www.vanessas.com

Another classic dumpling spot is Vanessa's. Though there are a few other locations in NYC, the one in Chinatown is the best, by a significant margin. Dumplings can be had on a plate or in soup; usually 8 are in an order for $4. Also available are sesame pancake sandwiches ($1 to $3), soups and noodle dishes.

## Joe's Shanghai

 J/Z/N/Q to Canal Street; B/D to Grand Street   212-233-8888

 Daily from to 11:00am to 11:00pm

 9 Pell Street   www.joeshanghairestaurants.com/ chinatownstore_eng.html

Founded in Queens, Joe's Shanghai has been in NYC since 1995. They've become famous for their soup dumplings, which are handcrafted and made to order. They come to the table in hot bamboo steamers in a light broth. Be careful biting into them abruptly, as you'll burn your mouth. One order is about $8.

## Vivi Bubble Tea

 J/Z/N/Q to Canal Street  212-566-6833

 Mondays to Thursdays from 10:00am to 9:30pm; Fridays to Saturdays from 10:00am to 10:30pm; Sundays from 10:00am to 10:00pm

 49 Bayard Street  www.vivibubbletea.com

This Taiwanese tea-based drink has become a hit in NYC in recent years. The popular drink consists of a thick drink with fruit or milk and the signature tapioca balls, which can be slurped through the over-sized plastic straws. Vivi's opened in 2007 and has been offering the classics, as well as innovative teas, to both Asian customers and others. From the Japanese Matcha to Cappuccino Milk tea, there is a wide variety of options that cater to range of palates.

# Accommodation

## Windsor Hotel

 www.windsorhotelnyc.com  212-226-3009

 108 Forsyth Street  B/D to Grand Street; J/Z to Bowery

This is a nice option in Chinatown that is cheaper than can be found in most of the surrounding areas. The rooms are basic and nothing fancy, but they're clean and get the job done for those that aren't looking to spend much time in the hotel. Rooms go from $190-$210 per night.

# Little Italy

*Although Little Italy has gotten progressively smaller over the years, its presence can certainly be felt. Since the original immigrants arrived and established businesses, there has been a slow and gradual decline of Italian presence.*

The major influx and expansion of Chinatown, as well as the expansion of the Lower East Side, have contributed to Little Italy's shrinking influence.

All that said, there are still a few blocks worth roaming that will give you the sense of what the more robust Little Italy was like not too long ago. Restaurant owners will greet you on the sidewalk and urge you to come and try their food.

The 11-day street fair in September of San Gennaro on Mulberry Street is a reminder of the legacy that Italian-Americans have had on NYC.

# Dining

## Rubirosa

 6 to Spring Street  212-965-0500

 Saturdays to Sundays 11:30am to 4:00pm; Sundays to Wednesdays 5:00pm to 11:00pm; Thursdays to Saturdays 5:00pm to midnight

 235 Mulberry Street  www.rubirosanyc.com

This restaurant opened after Joe and Pat's Pizzeria on Staten Island gained high recognition selling thin-crust pizza.

They sell pastas and meat, but most people come for the delicious pizza.

With options aside from the classic tomato and mozzarella, you can order a Vodka pizza, Sausage and Broccoli Rabe Pizza, or an Arugula Pizza with various cheese, vegetable, and meat add-ons ($18 to $30).

# La Mela

 J/Z to Bowery     212-431-9493

 11:30am to 2:00am

 167 Mulberry Street     www.lamelarestaurant.com

This classic Italian joint provides a festive and fun dinner option. Family-style menus are available for $25 per person. They'll bring an appetizer of fresh mozzarella and tomatoes, followed by hot antipasti and a range of pastas. Other prix-fixe options increase by about $10 adding more courses like Veal Francaise and Chicken Scarpariello. No matter how hungry you are, there is more than enough options to fill you up.

The place provides a homey environment with red and white-checkered tablecloths. It is a fun place to spend an evening.

# Ferrara Bakery

 J/Z to Bowery     212-226-6150

 Sundays to Thursdays from 8:00am to 10:00pm; Fridays to Saturdays from 8:00am to 12:00am midnight

 195 Grand Street     www.ferraranyc.com

This old Italian family bakery has its origins three generations back in 1892. It was a place where Italians would gather late at night after an opera, play some card games, drink espresso, and have some cannoli. Other classic Italian desserts are available – Napoleons, Éclairs, and Pasticcios, along with an array of Gelato flavors.

# Financial District

*The Financial District was where the interaction between colonizers and the original Native Americans that lived in present day Manhattan began. Now, it is the area of major financial institutions' headquarters.*

The New York Stock Exchange and the Federal Reserve Bank of New York are located on the southern tip of Manhattan, along with most NYC government offices.

The residential population has nearly doubled in size since the turn of the century, and it continues to grow. The narrow cobblestone streets are reminders of the old New York and the modern

glass skyscrapers are emblematic of the present day clientele. It's a wondrous place to wander around and consider how fast the whole city has developed.

## Attractions

### Museum of American Finance

 2/3 to Wall Street

 Adults: $8, Students and seniors: $5, Children (Under 6): Free

 Tuesdays to Saturdays from 10:00am to 4:00pm

 48 Wall Street

 www.moaf.org

This institution prides itself on being the only public museum focused on preserving, teaching, and displaying the history and importance of American finance. Permanent exhibitions explain the basics regarding financial markets, money, banking, and entrepreneurship.

### National Museum of the American Indian – New York

 4/5 to Bowling Green

 Free

 Daily from 10:00am to 5:00pm

 1 Bowling Green

 www.nmai.si.edu

Affiliated with the larger museum in Washington D.C., this Smithsonian Institution has exhibitions exploring the diversity of Native American people in the United States. The combination between permanent and temporary exhibitions provide everyone something to offer.

# 9/11 Memorial, Museum & One World Observatory

 A/C to Chambers or Fulton; E to World Trade Center; 1/2/3 to Chamber Streets; R to Cortlandt Street; 1/R to Rector Street

 See description.

 www.911memorial.org

 180 Greenwich Street

 See description.

The events of September 11, 2001, greatly changed NYC, and its residents have not forgotten it. In 2011, the memorial opened.

Michael Arad and Peter Walker's design, "Reflecting Absence" was chosen and construction began in 2006. The memorial consists of two one-acre pools with the largest man-made waterfalls in the United States.

The victims' names are inscribed on bronze plates that are attached to the walls of the pools. Other trees fill the rest of the 6 acres of the plaza.

In 2014, the Museum opened to the public. The exhibits have numerous images, artifacts, and oral histories of the people who lost their lives. In our opinion, it is the best museum we have ever visited anywhere in the world.

Finally, also located on-site is One World Trade Center, the tallest building in the US. At 1,776 feet tall, this building dominates NYC's skyline. On floors 100 to 102 you can visit the One World Observatory observation deck – standard tickets are $32.

**Pricing and Operating Hours:**
Memorial – Open: Daily from 7:30am to 9:00pm. Free Admission.

Museum – Open: Sun to Thurs from 9:00am to 8:00pm; Fri to Sat from 9:00am to 9:00pm. Free Admission: Tuesdays after 5:00pm. Other Days: Adults: $24, Seniors, Veterans and Students: $18, Ages 7 to 17: $15, Children 6 and under: Free.

Observatory – Open: Daily from 9:00am to 8:00pm. Adults: $32, Seniors $30 and Children $26.

## South Street Seaport

 2/3 to Fulton Street           Fulton Street

 www.southstreetseaport.com

This historic area on the East River has been used as a significant port since the mid 1600s.

Today, the South Street Seaport Museum can be viewed to learn about the history of the Seaport's importance. The whole area has also become a place for comprehensive entertainment. With stores, various places to eat, and opportunities to learn about the history, the South Street Seaport is an easy place to spend an entire morning or afternoon.

# Bowling Green Park

 4/5 to Bowling Green     Whitehall Street

 www.nycgovparks.org/parks/bowling-green

Bowling Green is NYC's oldest park with a rich history. It is next to the site of the original Dutch fort of New Amsterdam and the original 18th century fence is still standing, which surrounds the park. The park is well known for the bronze "Charging Bull" sculpture, which symbolizes intense financial optimism and prosperity. It was brought to the park in 1989 by guerilla artist Arturo Di Modica.

# Museum of Jewish Heritage

 1 to Rector Street; 4/5 to Bowling Green     Adults: $12, Seniors: $10, Students: $7, Under 12s: Free

 Sundays, Tuesdays, Thursdays from 10:00am to 5:45pm; Wednesdays from 10:00am to 8:00pm; Fridays from 10:00am to 5:00pm

 36 Battery Place     www.mjhnyc.org

This museum seeks to educate people about Jewish life before, during, and after the holocaust.

Exhibitions and collections are displayed year round to hone in on particular stories that are representative of Jewish culture.

All visitors will go through the entry rotunda and view a nine-minute multimedia presentation about the themes of the museum.

Then, you move on to peruse through parts of the 25,000-piece permanent collection as well as temporary exhibitions.

Free admission for all on Wednesdays from 4:00pm to 8:00pm

# Dining

## Delmonicos

 J/Z to Broad Street;
2/3 to Wall Street

 212-509-1144

 Mondays to Fridays from 11:30am to 10:00pm; Saturdays from
5:00pm to 10:00pm

 56 Beaver Street

 www.delmonicosrestaurantgroup.
com/restaurant/

Delmonico's began serving New Yorkers as early as 1827, selling pastries, coffee, wines, and liquors out of a small shop.

In the location it stands now, the family opened the first fine dining restaurant in the United States in 1837.

Now, it stands as a

classic Steak house selling Crab Cakes ($19), Roasted Oysters ($18), Roasted Halibut ($37) Double Cut Lamb Chops ($48), and a variety of steaks.

## Antinori Ristorante

 4/5 to Bowling Green;
N/R to Whitehall Street

 646-439-2200

 Daily from 6:00am to 11:00am; 12:00pm to 11:30pm

 8 Stone Street

 www.antinoriristorante.net

This Italian restaurant boasts a menu with various options so everyone can find something. Pasta is said to be their specialty, with wholewheat and gluten-free options to be topped with various fishes, meats, and vegetables.

## Blue Spoon Coffee

 2/3 to Fulton Street  212-809-8880

 Mondays to Thursdays from 7:00am to 6:30pm; Fridays from 7:00am to 6:00pm; Saturdays from 8:00am to 3:00pm

 90 William Street  www.bluespooncoffee.com

Since 2005, Blue Spoon Coffee has established itself as the best coffee shop in the neighborhood.

In addition to the standard coffee drinks they serve up sandwiches and hot pressed Paninis. Some offerings are Roasted, Turkey, and Swiss ($8.50) or House-made Hummus with roasted red peppers, greens, cucumbers, and plum tomatoes ($8).

Whether stopping in for a coffee or for a light lunch, this is a reliable option in the neighborhood.

## The Dead Rabbit Grocery and Grog

 N/R to Whitehall Street  626-422-7906

 Daily from 11:00am to 4:00pm

 30 Water Street  www.deadrabbitnyc.com

This two-floor establishment offers both a place to enjoy a nice craft beer or cocktail, as well as enjoy a solid and satisfying meal. The ground floor offers drinks while the upstairs serves small plates.

It has won a variety of awards like the Best American Cocktail Bar in 2014, and one of the world's 50 best bars in 2013 and 2014.

Vintage cocktails are done seasonally, and categorized as shaken, not stirred. They have clever names like "Doppelganger" – powers John's Lane Irish, aquavit, dry vermouth, yellow chartreuse, and celery bitters – or the "Hunger Striker" – brugal dry Dominican white rum, banks 5 island rum, dolin blanc, apple, saffron boston bitters, and vanilla ($15).

# Accommodation

## Gild Hall

 www.thompsonhotels.com/hotels/gild-hall

 212-232-7700

 15 Gold Street

 2/3 to Fulton Street

This luxury hotel option has rooms filled with leather indicative of designer Jim Walrods vision of creating a country house like feel. General rooms are between $400-$560 and the luxury suites go up to $1,500.

## Residence Inn

 http://www.marriott.com/hotels/travel/nycrl

 212-600-8900

 170 Broadway

 4/5 to Fulton Street

This brand new option opened in January of 2015 and offers a range of comfortable rooms in the heart of the financial district. A fitness room and complimentary breakfast are on site. Prices begin at $300 and go up to about $650.

## The Wall Street Inn

 www.thewallstreetinn.com

 877-747-1500

 9 S William Street

 4/5 to Bowling Green

This newly renovated building is set atop the lower Manhattan cobblestone streets and one of the oldest streets in Manhattan.

After a series of ownerships and fires, the current address was bought in the 1990s by Holocaust survivors and opened in 1999.

The rooms have marble tile baths, full-length mirrors, and are spacious. They are decorated with a classy style. Rooms are between $300-$400.

# Brooklyn

*Brooklyn has roots in some of the earliest battles in the Revolutionary War. George Washington tread over places like the Grand Army Plaza and Atlantic Avenue in order to push back some of the British troops.*

The village of Brooklyn was established in 1816 and people went back and forth between Manhattan on a ferry to Wall Street, to what is now Brooklyn Heights. For much of the 19th century, Brooklyn was considered to be a twin city of New York, geographically bigger than Manhattan, and highly populated.

When the Brooklyn Bridge was completed in 1883, the city merged with Manhattan to become NYC. The Brooklyn Navy Yard was an instrumental facility throughout World War II, and employed 70,000 people at its peak. Now there is a big mix of Brooklynites working in Brooklyn and Manhattan.

When people think of NYC, they generally think of the picturesque Manhattan – the skyline defined by the Empire State Building, Times Square, etc.

Even ten years ago, Brooklyn was a place tourists wouldn't visit, yet it also was a place Manhattanites avoided. However, in recent years, the borough has began to define itself as a separate city with a lot to offer. While population density may be associated with Manhattan, Brooklyn is the most populated borough in NYC with over 2.5 million people. And the diverse population brings a lot of flavor to the city.

The amount of time you have to spend in NYC will naturally effect how much of the outer boroughs you see, but if you have some time, exploring Brooklyn is worthwhile.

# Attractions

## Barclay's Center

 2/3/4/5/B/D/N/Q/R to Atlantic Avenue – Barclays Center

 620 Atlantic Avenue   www.barclayscenter.com

This multi-purpose indoor arena was built and argued over the course of many years but finally opened to the public in September of 2012.It is the home of the Brooklyn Nets basketball team, the hockey team, and the New York Islanders.

The design is modern and industrial, and from the exterior has a glass curtain wall with steel panels, intended to bring about the history and look of Brooklyn's brownstone apartments.

Various concerts and sporting events occur throughout the year.

# Brooklyn Bridge

 4/5/6 to Brooklyn Bridge; N/R City Hall; A/C High Street; F York Street

 www.nyc.gov/html/dot/html/infrastructure/brooklyn-bridge.shtml

The Brooklyn Bridge is, our opinion, one of the best sites to see in all of NYC. The Brooklyn Bridge is a unique fixture not just in New York, but also in the world.

The hybrid cable-stayed/suspension bridge was completed in 1883 and connects lower Manhattan to Dumbo and Brooklyn Heights.

The bridge itself is an architectural masterpiece, and unlike the two other bridges that connect Manhattan to Brooklyn – the Manhattan and the Williamsburg bridges – a subway does not run across, making it a quieter and more peaceful place to marvel at the lower Manhattan skyline. That is, if you ignore the traffic below.

Walking from Manhattan to Brooklyn, you can make your way to Brooklyn Bridge Park, which provides spectacular views of Manhattan at sunset.

The length of the bridge is 1.1 miles or 1.8 kilometers long. The bridge is open 24/7.

# Williamsburg

This neighborhood is said to be one of the epicenters of hipster culture and tends to embody gentrification. It has been home to many ethnic enclaves, and two in particular still maintain a presence – orthodox Jews and Puerto Ricans.

In the northern part of Williamsburg and eastwards there are mostly young white people, which has led to a lot of high-end vintage stores, unique eateries, and galleries opening up.

**Subway:** L to Bedford Avenue

# Prospect Park

Like Central Park, Prospect Park was designed by Frederick Law Olmsted. Although smaller in size, many argue Prospect Park is NYC's nicest public park.

Within the boundaries is the Prospect Park Zoo, a nature conservancy, a boathouse, and the Prospect Park Bandshell which hosts many free concerts during the summer.

Even as the weather gets nice and people in NYC flock to public parks, Prospect Park retains the intimacy and solitude that Central Park often lacks during beautiful weather.

## Coney Island

Between 1880 and World War II, Coney Island was the largest amusement area in the United States and attracted millions of people each year. There were three amusement parks, and the area became a resort destination for many. However, two main amusement parks faltered, but there was a resurgence in the 1970s.

Luna Park is now in operation today. There are newer rides but three main attractions are historical icons. The Wonder Wheel, a Ferris wheel built in 1918 holds 144 riders and still spins today. The Parachute Jump debuted at the 1939 World's Fair does not operate but can be viewed. And finally, the iconic roller coaster, The Cyclone, built in 1927 stands as the United States' oldest wooden roller coaster; it is still in operation today.

The other historical and iconic structure at Coney Island is the original site of Nathan's Hot Dogs. It is also the site where Nathan's Hot Dog Eating Contest has been held since 1972. Coney Island is no longer considered the resort destination it was built to be, especially with a large majority of the residents living in public housing. But if you have time, historically and culturally, it's a fascinating park of NYC.

**Subway:** D/F/N/Q to Coney Island – Stillwell Avenue

## Brooklyn Museum

 2/3 to Eastern Parkway

 Adults: $16, Students and seniors: $10, Children (19 and Under): Free

 Wednesdays 11:00am to 6:00pm; Thursdays 11:00am to 10:00pm; Fridays to Sundays 11:00am to 6:00pm;

 200 Eastern Parkway

 www.brooklynmuseum.org

With 1.5 million works in a space of 560,000 square feet, the Brooklyn Museum is NYC's second largest in size. There are substantial collections in the Egyptian Antiquities, as well as African, Oceanic, and Japanese art. Popular American artists represented are Mark Rothko, Georgia O'Keefe, Norman Rockwell, Edgar Degas, and others. Interesting temporary exhibits change year round.

Free admission on the first Saturday of the month.

# Dining

## Roberta's

 L to Morgan Avenue  718-417-1118

 Mondays to Fridays from 11:00am to midnight; Saturdays to Sundays from 10:00am to midnight

 261 Moore Street  www.robertaspizza.com

Situated in the warehouse, loft-apartment style neighborhood of Bushwick, many argue that this is one of the best pizza restaurants in all of NYC.

The Neapolitan-style pizza is made in a wood-burning oven with airy and crispy crust and fresh sauces and cheeses. You can order the simple originals ($14) or be a bit more daring and go for something like the Beatmaster – a pizza with tomato, mozzarella, gorgonzola, pork sausage, onions, capers, and jalapenos ($18).

## Torst

 G to Nassau Avenue  718-389-6034

 Sundays to Wednesdays midday to midnight; Thursdays from midday to 2:00am; Fridays to Saturdays from midday to 3:00am

 615 Manhattan Avenue  www.torstnyc.com

For those into beer, few better places can be found than Torst, a beer bar that opened in 2013 and has received high acclaim since.

On the border of Williamsburg and Greenpoint, the Danish-style bar has Scandavian chairs from the 1950s, and a high-tech glass-enclosed control panel under the taps so the bar stewards can calibrate the nitrogen and carbon dioxide mixes to make the compression perfect.

They have 21 beers on tap, which change regularly, and have over 200 beers by the bottle.

They also serve fresh-baked bread, cheese and meat plates, and a few sandwiches ($10 to $14).

## Junior's

 B/D/N/Q/R to
DeKalb Avenue

 718-852-5257

 Sundays to Thursdays from 6:30am to 12:00am midnight; Fridays to
Saturdays from 6:30am to 1:00am

 386 Flatbush Avenue
Extension

 www.juniorscheesecake.com

If you're walking through downtown Brooklyn, Junior's is a tough place to miss. There are a few other locations – in Grand Central, Times Square, and in Connecticut – but this is arguably the most important.

Harry Rosen worked with a baker to create "The World's Most Fabulous Cheesecake" based on a family recipe. In 1950, he opened Junior's.

They serve soups, salads, sandwiches, and more, but they're most well known for their desserts.

## Diner

 J/M/Z to Marcy
Avenue

 718-486-3077

 Mondays to Fridays 11:00am to 5:00pm, 6:00pm to 12:00am midnight;
Saturdays & Sundays 10:00am to 1:00pm, 6:00pm to 1:00am

 85 Broadway

 www.dinernyc.com

Opening in 1999 in a Kullman train car underneath the Williamsburg Bridge, Diner is emblematic of the old-new feelings of the area.

The menus change daily and use only the fresh ingredients.

Items in the past have included pork croquettes over creamy grits with fried eggs, watercress, and salsa, and a beef burger ($15).

# Buttermilk Channel

 F/G to Smith Street   718-852-8490

 Mon to Wed 5:00pm to 10:00pm; Thurs 5:00pm to 11:00pm; Fri 5:00pm to midnight; Saturdays & Sundays 10:00pm to 3:00am

 524 Court Street   www.buttermilkchannelnyc.com

Buttermilk Channel is named after the strait between Brooklyn and Governors Island – a prior dairy-farming mecca. Doug Crowell, the owner and the graduate of the Culinary Institute of America, and Chefs Ryan Angulo and Jon Check have crafted menus that bring new flavors to more traditional bistro and American fare.

# La Superior

 L to Bedford Avenue   718-388-5988

 Sundays to Thursdays from 12:00pm midday to 12:00am midnight; Fridays to Saturdays from 12:00pm midday to 2:00am

 295 Berry Street   www.lasuperiornyc.com

An unassuming place on the south side of Williamsburg, La Superior serves up high-quality Mexican fare with modern twists.

A variety of tacos are on the menu, with fillings like Tinga de pollo – shredded chicken in chipotle tomato sauce – or Camaron al chipotle – sautéed shrimp with chipotle. They also serve common Mexico City street food such as Gorditas – mixed chorizo and cheese, served with lettuce and Mexican cream.

# Queens

*Like Brooklyn, Queens was its own city and county until its incorporation to NYC as a borough in 1807. During the American Revolution, Queens remained relatively untouched. When the Queensboro Bridge was finished in 1909, transportation between Queens and Manhattan became more accessible, and more people began commuting between the two boroughs.*

In 1939, Queens was the site of the New York Word's Fair and LaGuardia Airport opened. JFK Airport opened in 1948 and Queens again hosted the New York World's Far in 1964, bringing more and more visitors to the borough.

Today, Queens is the most ethnically diverse urban area in the world. Nearly 50% of the population is foreign born, creating strong ethnic enclaves where New Yorkers and tourists, should they decide, can experience a wide range of cultures.

## Attractions

### Astoria

For most of the 19th and early 20th century, Astoria saw an influx of Irish, Italian, and Jewish immigrants into the neighborhood. When the 1960s rolled around, a large number of Greeks and immigrants from Cyprus came into the area, opening up restaurants and bakeries that exist today. In more recent years, the Arab population has been growing. Thus, on every street corner there are new odors to smell, new foods to taste, and different people to talk to.

**Subway**: N/Q to Broadway

### Museum of the Moving Image

 M/R to Steinway Street

 Adults: $12, Students and seniors: $9, Ages 3 to 12: $6, Under 3s: Free

 Wednesdays to Thursdays from 10:30am to 5:00pm; Fridays from 10:30am to 8:00pm; Saturdays to Sundays from 11:30am to 7:00pm

 36-01 35th Avenue

 www.movingimage.us

This museum is the only in the United States that is dedicated to all aspects of moving images. From the art, history, technique, and technology, exhibits encompass a wide range of subjects and the collection is unique and for people of all ages.

# Socrates Sculpture Park

 N/Q to Broadway      Free

 Daily from 10:00am to sunset

 32-01 Vernon Boulevard      www.socratessculpturepark.org

Socrates Sculpture Park is situated on land that was an abandoned landfill and illegal dumpsite. It was founded in 1986, as the first space dedicated to exhibiting large-scale sculptures. The park is right on the east River and on a nice day is a great place for a picnic

## Flushing

While Manhattan certainly boasts a noteworthy Chinatown, the Chinese-immigrant population of Flushing, Queens, is far denser, insular, and more robust. This is a place to go to get a real taste for what its like to live in an Asian city. You'll find authentic cuisine, rare Japanese anime editions, and much more.

**Subway**: 7 to Flushing – Main Street

## Flushing Meadows – Corona Park

The fourth biggest public park in NYC, Flushing Meadows contains the USTA Billie Jean King National Tennis Center, The Met's Citi Field, the New York Hall of Science, the Queens Museum of Art, the Queens Wildlife Center, and other features.

It was also the location of the 1939 and 1964 World's Fair, and the enormous sculptural Unispheres can still be viewed in the park. On weekends families will bring barbecue food, soccer/footballs, and other games to spend the day.

**Subway**: 7 to 111 Street

## The Noguchi Museum

Based on a Japanese-American artist, Isamu Noguchi, this museum is situated in an old industrial building with an open-air sculpture garden and reflective space to contemplate the works. The collection exhibits a range of sculptures, portraits, drawings, designs, lunar projects, and more. On the first Friday of every month admission is free.

 N/Q to Broadway

 Wednesdays to Fridays from 10:00am to 5:00pm; Saturdays to Sundays from 11:00am to 6:00pm

 9-01 33rd Road

 Adults: $10, Students and seniors: $5, Children (Under 12): Free

 www.noguchi.org

## MoMA PS1

If you're interested in experimental art, there is no better place to go than MoMA PS1. One of the oldest and largest nonprofit contemporary art institutions in the United States, the art exhibited at MoMA PS1 will challenge your notions of what it means for something to be art.

 E/M to Court Sqaure-23rd Street; 7 to Court Square

 Adults: $10, Students and seniors: $5, Children (Under 16): Free

 Mondays, Thursdays from midday to 6:00pm

 22-25 Jackson Avenue

 www.momaps1.org

# Dining

## Taverna Kyclades

 N/Q to Astoria – Ditmars Boulevard     718-545-8666

 Mondays to Thursdays from 12:00pm midday to 11:00pm; Fridays to Saturdays from midday to 11:30pm; Sundays from midday to 10:30pm

 33-07 Ditmars Boulevard     www.tavernakyclades.com

If you do find yourself in Astoria and get a hankering for some Greek food most restaurants in the area are good bets.

However, Taverna Kyclades has a reputation that exceeds many others.

Classic Greek staples like stuffed grape leaves ($6.75) or spinach pie ($7.50) can be shared as appetizers.

For entrees many opt for the meats, like a Chicken Kebab with lemon potatoes ($14.50) or fresh grilled fish.

## The Queens Kickshaw

 M/R to Steinway Street     718-777-0913

 Mondays to Thursdays 7:30am to 12:00am midnight; Fridays 7:30am to 1:00am; Saturdays 9:00am to 1:00am; Sundays 9:00am to 12:00am

 40-17 Broadway     www.thequeenskickshaw.com

This niche spot serves specialty coffees, beer, and grilled cheese sandwiches.

Most of their beers and products come from local sources, in the NYC area. Their draught options change on a regular basis, but they always have over 25 beers to choose from that are from all over the world.

By way of food, they serve shared plates like Cider Cheese with Soft Pretzels ($8.50), or heart soups like the Broccoli Soup ($8). They have other entrees but are known for five different grilled cheese sandwiches with different ingredients mixed in like vegetables, hummus, jam, and other ($9 to $12).

# Mustang Thakali Kitchen

 E/F/M/R to Jackson Heights – Roosevelt; 7 to 74th Street – Broadway

 Mondays to Fridays from 11:00am to 11:00pm; Saturdays to Sundays from midday to midnight

 74-14 37th Avenue　　　 718-898-5088

Jackson Heights is one of the most diverse neighborhoods in NYC and has dense enclaves of South Americans, as well as South and East Asians. Naturally, numerous good and authentic ethnic eateries are available.

One such restaurant is Mustang Thakali Kitchen. With an unassuming storefront, this establishment has made a name for its delicious Nepalese delicacies.

Most entrees come with a clump of rice in the middle surrounded by a combination of different stews. The popular lassi drinks offset some of the spices.

## New World Mall Food Court

 7 to Flushing – Main Street　　 718-353-0551

 Daily from 9:00am to 10:00pm

 136-20 Roosevelt Avenue　　 www.newworldmallny.com

The mall – the largest indoor Asian Market in the State of New York has 108 retail shops, an enormous Asian Supermarket, and a food cart serving 32 different Asian foods from throughout the continent.

Bright lights, a hectic atmosphere, and foods and smells that look entirely unfamiliar to most fill the mall, providing a truly unique cultural experience.

# The Bronx

*Named after the Bronx River, the Bronx was originally part of Westchester County until the latter part of the 19th century. When the City of New York was established in 1898, the Bronx became a borough. In the beginning of the 20th century, the area was a manufacturing hub. In 1919 the Bronx had 63 piano factories alone.*

The population grew rapidly, along with the manufacturing industry, until the 1950s. After World War I, residential construction increased and Irish, Italian, and Jewish Americans began settling in the area.

However, after World War II and the Great Depression, the borough began an economic decline and an increase in crime and poverty.

Since the 1980s, revitalization and development has begun to take place in the borough and the Bronx is seen to be on a continuous rise.

Even though one fifth of the area of the Bronx is made up by parkland, it is still the third most densely populated county in the United States.

It's known for being the "Birthplace of Hip Hop" and the home of Yankee fans.

# Attractions

### Bronx Brewery

 6 to Cypress Avenue     718-402-1000

 Wednesdays to Fridays at 3:00pm; Saturdays to Sundays at 12:00pm

 856 E 136th Street     www.thebronxbrewery.com

Most people go to the Brooklyn Brewery if they're planning on visiting a Brewery in NYC. However, the Tasting Room and outdoor Backyard make the Bronx Brewery a tough competitor.

You can visit the brewery, do tastings, and carry out some pints. Since the official launch in 2011, the brewery has grown rapidly and increased its distribution.

## Bronx Zoo

 2/5 to Bronx Park East

 Adults: $20, Seniors: $18, Children: $13, Under 2s: Free

 Mondays to Fridays from 10:00am to 5:00pm; Saturdays to Sundays from 10:00am to 5:30pm

 2300 Southern Boulevard

 www.bronxzoo.com

This 265-acre facility of wildlife and habitats is the perfect urban escape, especially for those with kids. Popular exhibits like Tiger Mountain, Himalayan Highlands, Congo Gorilla Forest, and the World of Reptiles are geared towards entertaining all ages.

## Botanical Gardens

 B/D to Kingsbridge Road

 Tuesdays to Sundays from 10:00am to 6:00pm

 Weekdays – Adults: $20, Students & seniors: $18, Under 12s: $8, Under 2s: Free; Weekends – Adults: $25, Students & seniors: $22, Under 12s: $10, Under 2s: Free

 2900 Southern Boulevard

 www.nybg.org

Since its founding in 1891, the Botanical Garden has been the perfect oasis outside of the NYC metropolis.

There are 250 acres to browse through with plants and flora that exist in a variety of climates.

You'll be able to smell the odors and see the textures of tropical, desert, and temperate botany.

## The Edgar Allan Poe Cottage

 B/D to Kingsbridge Road

 Adults: $6, Students and seniors: $5

 Sundays from 11:00am to 5:00pm; Tuesdays to Saturdays from 10:00am to 5:00pm

 1914-16 East Main Street     www.poemuseum.org

For those interested in literary history, the Edgar Allan Poe Museum may be an interesting day trip. Opened in 1922, this old stone house is just a few blocks away from the notoriously dark writer's first Richmond home. The museum has a collection of Poe's manuscripts, letters, first editions, and other belongings.

# Dining

### Enzo's Italian Restaurant

 5 to Morris Park     718-409-3828

 Tuesday to Saturday from midday to 10:00pm and Sunday from 1:00pm to 9:00pm. Closed Monday.

 1998 Williamsbridge Road     www.enzosbronxrestaurant.com

Although some think of Manhattan when they hear about Little Italy, other New Yorkers think of Arthur Avenue in the Bronx.

Generations of Italian families in the area have kept businesses and restaurants with traditional Italian fare. Enzo's is one of the best.

The food is traditional, Eggplant Rollatini ($11), Bistecca Milanese ($26), and Penne alla Vodka ($18), and made with the freshest ingredients.

## Patina African Kitchen

 2/5 to Freeman Street   718-378-7700   823 E 169th Street

This restaurant is one of many West African restaurants in the Borough. This particular cuisine is Nigerian, made by a woman who grew up in Lagos and came to NYC in 1988. She serves up favorites like Egusi – a combination of spinach and ground melon seeds.

Most dishes come with homemade hot sauces and other pepper-based dishes.

## 188 Bakery Chuchifritos

 B/D to Fordham Road   718-367-4500   168 E 188th Street

This Puerto Rican diner makes some of the best Mofongo – a dish of fried plantains decorated with meats and other stews. Typical toppings include cheese, pork chops, or chicharrones ($8).

Other Puerto Rican beloved staples bring together numerous locals of both Puerto Rican descent and otherwise.

## The Good Dine

 2/5 to 219th Street   718-325-3463   3922 White Plains Road

Said to be the Bronx's best Jamaican restaurant (and one of many) is The Good Dine. The plate of Oxtail is particularly well-renowned ($7 to $12). Other combinations of rice, beans, and meats often are cooked with fiery spices.

The storefront of this unassuming dining spot should not deter you; the take out food containers contain some of the best Caribbean food in the whole city.

# Staten Island

*Often the most neglected and forgotten borough is Staten Island. Even prior to colonization, the tribe that inhabited the land of Staten Island was a separate division of the larger Lenape people. The island later became an important territory during the Revolutionary War, as the British took control of the land.*

In 1776, 140 British ships arrived on Staten Island to launch an invasion of New York. The Battle of Staten Island occurred in 1777 with inconclusive outcomes and the British inhabited the island until their final evacuation in 1783.

As with the rest of the boroughs, the towns of Staten Island disappeared and it became a borough in 1898.

The Verrazano-Narrows Bridge was completed in 1964 and connected Staten Island to New Jersey, and Brooklyn. This led to a significant population growth on the Island throughout the next few decades.

Staten Island is known for its natural habitats. Fresh Kills, a freshwater estuary, and other wetlands have been designated a Significant Coastal Fish and Wildlife Habitat. The Freshkills Park was a project implemented after 9/11, which is being built over public landfill.

Significant Italian, Russian, Polish, and Sri Lankan communities reside throughout he Island, as do a few other ethnic groups.

# Attractions

## Historic Richmond Town

 Oakwood Heights

 Adults: $8, Students and seniors: $6, Children (4 to 11): $5

 Wednesdays to Sundays 1:00pm to 5:00pm. Closed Mondays & Tuesdays

 441 Clarke Avenue

 www.historicrichmondtown.org

This preserved historic town and farm with artifacts and structures from the 17th century sits in the middle of the island. For two centuries Richmond was the government center of Staten Island, known as Richmond County until 1898.

This old preserved area is an odd glimpse into what life was like over one hundred years ago. Guided tours are at 2:30pm Wednesday to Friday, and at 2:00pm and 3:30pm on Saturday and Sunday.

## The Staten Island Ferry

 1 to South Ferry           Free

 Every 15 to 30 minutes, 24 hours per day

 4 Whitehall Street           www.siferry.com

The Staten Island Ferry is not only the most convenient way to get from Manhattan to the island, but it is also an event in and of itself. If you go at sunset, the views of Manhattan, the Statue of Liberty, and Ellis Island are particularly magnificent. If you can time it so you're riding the Ferry at sunset, prepare yourself for an idyllic setting.

## Freshkills Park

www.freshkillspark.org

With 2,200 acres, Freshkills Park is nearly three times the size of Central Park.

In 2001 the planning began to create a massive green space over a former landfill. Though the park is not fully complete (and won't be until the 2030s), much of it is up and running and there are significant opportunities for outdoor recreation.

## Sailor's Snug Harbor

 1000 Richmond Terrace     www.snug-harbor.org

This area was founded to be a relaxation spot for retired sailors in 1801. All in all, this area consists of 26 historic buildings, nine botanical gardens, a two-acre urban farm, and 10 acres of wetlands. It is a place where a variety of culture is presented and comes together. From architecture to visual art, to theater, to dance, to music, to environmental science, a lot can be found.

Exhibitions and performances change throughout the year. Hours and admissions vary depending on the sites.

# Dining

## Denino's Pizzeria and Tavern

 Sundays to Thursdays 11:00am to 11:00pm; Fridays to Saturdays 11:00am to 11:45pm     718-442-9401

 524 Port Richmond Avenue     www.deninos.com

This family owned establishment opened as a Tavern shortly after the repeal of Prohibition in 1937. In 1951, they began serving pizza and by the 1990s began gaining critical acclaim for serving the best pizza in all of NYC.

While they serve a few platters, meatball heroes and salads, everyone comes for the pizzas: the thin crust pizza with endless toppings is unbeatable.

## Jade Island

 Mon to Thurs 11:30am to 11:00pm; Fri 11:30am to midnight; Sat 12:30pm to midnight; Sundays from 12:30am to 11:00pm     718-761-8080

 2845 Richmond Avenue     jadeislandstaten.com

This restaurant is quite the spectacle. It's a dark, spacious area, with a tropical motif. Staff wear Hawaiian shirts and serve sugary drinks. On the small menu are Americanized Chinese staples. It is so over the top and goofy that you're bound to have a good time.

# Shopping

*As well as being filled with museums, fantastic places to eat and amazing accommodation, New York City is also a world-class city for shopping. Many call it the shopping capital of the world, and you will find a multitude of places to shop – no matter your taste or budget.*

The main shopping locations for most visitors will be: Times Square where there are big high-street brand names such as Disney, American Eagle and M&Ms; Fifth Avenue where you will find upmarket and designer brands such as Abercrombie, Apple, Tiffany and Co. and Dolce and Gabbana; and Madison Avenue for true luxury brands such as Tom Ford, Missoni, Alexander McQueen, Hermès and Valentino.

As well as the aforementioned locations, large department stores such as Macy's and Bloomingdale's should be on shopaholics' must-do lists.

However, whether you are strolling through Chinatown or Queens, there is a shopping opportunity round every corner of this city. This section lists some of the city's best shopping locations that we think you cannot miss.

## Bloomingdale's

 4/5/6/N/Q/R to 59 St – Lexington Av

 212-705-2000

 9:00am to 10:00pm daily

 59th Street and Lexington Avenue

 www.bloomingdales.com

This is one of the most famous department stores in NYC.

Brands on offer here include ALLSAINTS, AQUA, Burberry, Michael Kors, MARC JACOBS, Ralph Lauren, as well as hundreds more.

This is also the place to get the fashionable 'little' and 'medium brown bags' that so many carry around the city.

Whether it is high-end fashion, kids toys, home items, or luxury handbags, it is all at Bloomingdale's.

# Macy's

 A/C/E/1/2/3/B/D/F/V/N/Q/ R/W to 34 Street

 212-695-4400

 Daily from 8:00am to 11:00pm or midnight. On Thursdays Macy's opens slightly later at 9:30am.

 151 W 34th Street

 www.macys.com

Macy's is one of the most famous locations in New York, and up until 2009 this was the world's largest department store.

Some of the brands in Macy's include Tomy Hilfiger, MAC, Martha Stewart Collection, 32 Degrees, Polo Ralph Lauren, Charter Club, Calvin Klein, Lacoste Home and Lancôme.

You can find vouchers online for a 10% discount off most of the store. Macy's goes full out for the Christmas season, so if you are visiting then, there's even more joy. The window displays year-round are something to be admired too.

# Saks Fifth Avenue

 B/D/F/V to 47-50/Rockefeller Center, or E/6 to 51 Street/Lexington Avenue

 212-753-4000

 Monday to Saturday from 9:30am to 9:00pm, Sunday from 10:00am to 8:30pm

 611 Fifth Avenue

 saksfifthavenue.com

Founded in 1898, Saks is steeped in history and is still one of the most visited and largest department stores in New York City. This high-end location features well-known designer brands here include Burberry, Diane von Furstenberg, Dolce & Gabbana, Givenchy, Jimmy Choo, Prada, and Valentino, amongst many others.

## Barneys New York

 4/5/6 to 59 St – Lexington, Av or N/Q/R to Lexington Av/59 St

 212-826-8900

 Mon to Fri 10:00am to 8:00pm, Sat 10:00am to 7:00pm, and Sun 11:00am to 7:00pm

 660 Madison Avenue

 www.barneys.com

This is a relatively new addition to the department store line-up in NYC, having opened in 1993.

The store is 275,000 square feet and is another high-end department store.

Notable brands include Saint Lauren Paris, The Row, Burberry Prorsum and Thom Browne.

## Century 21

 R to Cortlandt Street or 4/5 to Fulton Street

 212-227-9092

 Mon to Fri 7:45am to 10:00pm, Sat 8:00am to 10:00pm, Sun 10:00am to 10:00pm

 21 Dey Street

 www.c21stores.com

This New York City-based department store chain focuses on more affordable mid-range offerings than some of the aforementioned department stores.

There are still many designer brands and Century 21 really focuses on providing big discounts, usually of 40% to 70% off the standard retail price.

From clothing to housewares, and electronics to cosmetics, there is a lot of choice.

## Apple Store

 4/5/6 to 59 St – Lexington, Av or N/Q/R to Lexington Av/59 St

 212-336-1440

 24/7

 www.apple.com

 767 5th Avenue

Probably the most famous technology store in the world, the Apple Store's cubic entrance is recognized around the world. Inside, this is just like any other Apple Store with the opportunity to purchase Mac and iOS products, as well as a Genius bar for any issues, and regular tutorials and classes. The store is open 24 hours a day, 7 days a week.

# Hershey's Chocolate World

 N/Q/R to 49 Street

 212-581-9100

 9:00am to midnight daily

 1593 Broadway

 www.hersheys.com/visit-us/times-square.aspx

From the famous chocolate kisses to jumbo candy bars, there is something for every chocolate fan at Hershey's.

# Maison Goyard

 F to Lexington Av - 63 St

 212-813-0005

 Monday to Saturday 10:00am to 6:00pm, Closed on Sundays

 20 E 63rd St

 www.goyard.com/en/store

Until recently the only place you could purchase Goyard products was from small boutique sellers, but now Goyard has its own "maison" or home. Inside, it is Parisian-styled, yet with a distinct twist of New York elegance too. If designer handbags and luxury one-off accessories are your thing, then look no further.

## M&Ms World

 N/Q/R to 49 Street  212-295-3850

 9:00am to 1:00am daily, except Sundays when it closes at midnight

 1600 Broadway  www.mmsworld.com/locations.aspx

The same concept as the Hershey's store on the previous page, but for M&Ms. This store is directly opposite Hersheys. Personally, we prefer this store to Hershey's because it feels easier to move around as it is bigger. There is a wider variety of merchandise here too and (importantly) we prefer M&Ms chocolate.

## Abercrombie & Fitch

 E/M to 5 Av – 53 Street, or F to 57 Street  212-306-0936

 Monday to Saturday from 10:00am to 8:00pm, Sunday from 11:00am to 7:00pm.

 720 Fifth Avenue  www.abercrombie.com

Loved by teens and young twenty-somethings, Abercrombie has made its name through its athletic-fitted clothing that sticks to classic styles. The Fifth Avenue location is the company's flagship store which is famous for its high-priced clothing and attractive model-style employees. If you are looking for a bargain, visit the Fulton Street location, as the flagship store does not hold sales.

## Tiffany & Co.

 E/M to 5 Av – 53 Street, or F to 57 Street  212-755-8000

 Monday, Thursday, Friday and Saturday 9:30am to 9:00pm, Tuesday and Wednesday 10:00am to 8:00pm, Sunday 11:00am to 7:00pm

 727 Fifth Avenue  www.tiffany.com

This is Tiffany's flagship retail location and has stood here since 1940. If diamonds are your best friend, you undoubtedly know that there is simply no better place to shop at in the world. As an added bonus to this beautiful store, you can see the original Tiffany Diamond on display on the main floor here.

# The Strand Bookstore

 4/5/6/L/N/Q/R/L to Union Square

 212-473-1452

 Monday to Saturday 9:30am to 10:30pm, Sunday 11:00am to 10:30pm

 828 Broadway

 www.strandbooks.com

Booklovers need look no further than The Strand. Their collection of over 2.5 million items and 18 miles of bookshelves, means that you are bound to find something for the flight back home here. There is a rare books room filled with antique reads.

# Chelsea Market

 A/C/E to 14 Street

 212-652-2110

 Monday to Saturday 7:00am to 9:00pm, Sunday from 8:00am to 8:00pm

 75 Ninth Avenue

 www.chelseamarket.com

Located not too far from the Hudson River, and with the Highline passing through it, Chelsea Market is a must-see location which provides a sensory overload unlike anywhere else in the city. It is a food hall and shopping mall in one space, and is a joy to explore and some of the food is simply delightful. Here you forget that you are in a city with skyscrapers and feel like you are at a local market in any small town.

Foods of NY Tours (www.foodsofny.com) runs paid-for tours of the market four times daily: these include tastes of some of the food on offer.

One of the most well-known locations inside the market is 'Artists & Fleas' where vendors sell handmade crafts, antiques, vintage clothing, jewelry and more.

# Nightlife

*Known as the city that never sleeps, NYC has plenty to offer during the evening. Whether you want a casual drink, a club to party the night away, live music or theatre and musical performances, there is something for every type of night owl. This section lists our favorite locations to spend an evening out in the city.*

## Bars/Lounges/Pubs/Clubs

### Upstairs NYC Rooftop Bar and Lounge

 6 to 51 Street or E/M to Lexington Av/53 St

 212-702-1600

 Monday to Wednesday 5:00pm to 1:00am, Thursday and Friday 5:00pm to 2:00am, closed on Saturday, Sunday midday to 11:00pm

 145 E 50th St

 www.upstairsnyc.com

This bar provides some fantastic views of Midtown Manhattan and the famous Chrysler building from the 30th story. There are indoor and outdoor areas, and the bar serves small bites, as well as alcoholic and non-alcoholic beverages. This place oozes chic. The dress code requires business casual dress, with no sneakers, caps of flip flops accepted. Signature cocktails run about $18, glasses of wine are $15 to $22, sides and sliders are $11 to $24.

### The 13th Step

 6 to Astor Place

 212-228-8020

 Daily from 11:30am to 4:00am

 149 2nd Ave

 www.nycbestbar.com

This huge bar has a very college-like vibe to it, and therefore is very popular with the younger crowd. If you're a sports fan, like beer pong, and like a frat-like atmosphere, this may just be the perfect place for you.

Cocktails are much more affordable than at high-end bars, and regular happy hours and daily specials means you can get beers as low as $1 and shots from $4.

Mixed drinks are $7 too, making this a bargain place to drink. The bar food is cheap and plentiful too.

## Dive Bar

 1/2/3 to 96 Street  212-749-4358

 Daily from 11:30am to 4:00am

 732 Amsterdam Ave  www.divebarnyc.com

A good local's joint with a large choice of beers, as well whiskeys/scothches, with good bar food. The staff are friendly and the atmosphere is great.

This is a great place to hang out for a few hours, and sports games are often shown too.

Despite its name, this isn't your typical 'dive bar' and the quality of service, drink and food is pretty great!

## Le Bain

 A/C/E to 14 St  212-645-7600

 Monday 4:00pm to midnight, Tuesday to Thursday 4:00pm to 4:00am, Friday and Saturday 2:00pm to 4:00am, and Sunday 2:00pm to 3:00am

 444 W 13th Street  www.standardhotels.com/new-york/features/le-bain

This bar/club combo features indoor and outdoor areas, with three hot tubs in total (one inside, two outside) which are open during the summer season. It is located on the top floor of The Standard High Line hotel. The crowd is generally very friendly, and who wouldn't be when there's a crêpe stand on the dance floor? The views are great from this rooftop location. Mixed drinks are $14 here. Bring a bathing suit/shorts if you fancy swimming.

## Cielo

 A/C/E to 14 St  646-543-8556

 Monday to Saturday from 11:00am to 7:00pm and 10:00pm to 4:00am. Closed on Sunday

 18 Little W 12th St  www.cieloclub.com

If you're a fan of techno, electronic and house music, this is the place for you. The club's sound system is one of the best we've heard in NYC. Cielo is, however, quite small as far as clubs go, and the cover charge can be high – ask before getting in line. Get a guest DJ, though, and the atmosphere can be electric.

# Live Music

## Madison Square Garden

 1/2/3/A/C/E to 34 St – Penn Station

 212-465-6741

 4 Pennsylvania Plaza

 www.thegarden.com

This is perhaps NYC's most famous multi-purpose venue, showing sports, as well as live concerts with a capacity of 20,000 people. Conveniently located in the heart of Manhattan, and with good transportation links, this is the place of choice for major artists when playing in NYC.

## Bowery Ballroom

 B/D to Grand Street; F/J/M/Z to Essex/Delancey Street

 212-260-4700

 6 Delancey Street

 www.boweryballroom.com

Many say this is the perfect-sized venue in New York, not too small but big enough to get great artists to host here. There are three levels to this venue providing different atmospheres, and levels of intimacy. This is one of our favorite venues in the city.

## Mercury Lounge

 F to 2nd Avenue or Delancey Street

 212-260-4700

 217 E Houston St

 www.mercuryloungenyc.com

This is a great place for up and coming bands, and with a capacity of only 250 people, it is tiny and intimate. Ticket and drink prices are affordable by New York standards.

## Irving Plaza

 N/Q/R/4/5/6/L to Union Square

 212-777-6800

 17 Irving Place

 http://venue.irvingplaza.com

This venue is well located and is a decent size. The sound system is good at this place but the entire venue is standing room with no seats, which may be a problem for some. Some of the greatest acts of all-time have played here including U2, Eric Clapton and the Beastie Boys. This is another of our favorite venues in town.

# Theater

A visit to NYC would not be complete without taking in one of the stunning productions on Broadway.

Whether it is a musical, historical drama or a thriller, there is a show for everyone. Off-Broadway productions are also available, but here we will focus on some of the top shows in the city at the moment.

**Buying tickets:**
To book theater tickets, you can either do so in advance over the phone or online, in person at the box office or you can visit one of the numerous ticket resellers. If there is a show that you absolutely MUST see, the best option is to book online where you can often even choose specific seats and have an idea of what your view of the stage will be like.

**Discounted last-minute tickets:**
If you can wait until you are in NYC, you can get great deals on many Broadway shows by visiting one of the TKTS booths (www.tdf.org).

The website will give you an idea of what tickets are currently on sale at the booths so you can have an idea of what shows regularly have discounted tickets. A TKTS app with live times is also available. You cannot get these tickets online or over the phone, but only in person.

TKTS sells tickets for major shows at up to 50% off the regular price on the day of performance. There are three locations: Times Square, South Street Seaport and Downtown Brooklyn. The Times Square location is generally the busiest. Check online for opening times and get there early (before opening) to get the best choice of tickets.

## Aladdin

|  1/2/3/7/A/C/E/N/Q/R/S to Times Square |  866-870-2717 |
| --- | --- |
|  New Amsterdam Theatre, 214 West 42nd Street |  www.aladdinthemusical.com |

Disney's hit movie is now playing on Broadway! With rave reviews from critics, a hilarious genie and incredible sets, this is one show that is sure to spellbind the whole family.

## The Book of Mormon

|  C/E/1 to 50 St or N/Q/R to 49 St |  212-560-2197 |
| --- | --- |
|  Eugene O'Neill Theatre, 230 W 49th Street |  www.bookofmormonbroadway.com |

Winner of 9 Tony awards, including for Best Musical, The Book of Mormon is based on the Latter Day Saint's religious book and first opened in 2011. Since then it has made millions laugh.

## The Color Purple

|  A/C/E to 42 St - Port Authority Bus Terminal |  212-239-6200 |
| --- | --- |
|  Bernard B Jacobs Theatre, 242 W 45th St |  www.colorpurple.com |

Based on the incredibly moving novel by Alice Walker, 'The Color Purple' has made its US stage debut on Broadway. Starring multi-award-winner Jennifer Hudson and Cynthia Erivo who was part of the London cast, this is one tear-jerker of a show.

# The Lion King

 1/2/3/7/N/Q/ R/S to Times Square – 42 St

 The Minskoff Theatre, 200 W 45th St

212-869-0550

www.lionking.com

Disney's 'The Lion King' retells the story of the hit movie through stunning animal puppets, incredible singing, and sets which transport you to East Africa. The show is top-earning title in box-office history having raked in over $6 billion in worldwide ticket sales.

# The Phantom of the Opera

 A/C/E to 42 St - Port Authority Bus Terminal

 The Majestic Theatre, 247 West 44th Street

212-239-6200

www.thephantomoftheopera.com

Andrew Lloyd Webber's hit musical is the longest-running on Broadway, and over 25 years later this stunning masterpiece entrances audiences young and old. The costumes are stunning, the story and score unforgettable, and the set changes here have to be seen to be believed.

# Wicked

 C/E/1 to 50th Street

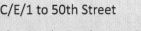 

212-586-6510

 The Gershwin Theatre, 222 W 51st Street

 www.wickedthemusical.com

This spellbinding musical retells the story behind the Wicked Witch of the West from "The Wizard of Oz". Through this funny and elaborate journey, we discover why she acts the way she does. Be prepared for beautiful costumes, elaborate sets and incredibly memorable musical numbers in one of our favorite shows on Broadway.

# Chicago

 N/Q/R to 49 St or C/E to 50 St

 The Ambassador Theatre, 219 W 39th Street

 212-239-6200

 www.chicagothemusical.com

The longest-running American musical in Broadway history, running for over 20 years, Chicago is incredible. This satirical musical retells the story of celebrity criminals and the justice system.

## Hamilton

 A/C/E to 42 St - Port Authority Bus Terminal

 Richard Rodgers Theatre, 226 W 46th St

 212-221-1211

 www.hamiltonbroadway.com

This new musical from Lin-Manuel Miranda retells the story of Alexander Hamilton, one of the founding fathers of the USA. With a unique score with samples from Notorious B.I.G., this is a patriotic show that is fast becoming a Broadway hit.

## Les Misérables

 1/2/3/7/N/Q/R/S to Times Square – 42 St

 Imperial Theatre, 249 West 45th Street

 212-239-6200

 www.lesmis.com/broadway

This world-renowned musical, based on Frenchman Victor Hug's novel, is a whirlwind of a tale during the French revolution. The show has won over 100 major awards, including Oliviers, Tonys and Grammys, and still regularly breaks Box Office records.

# Seasonal Events

*No matter what time of the year you visit, there is always something different and unique going on in the city. Here we cover some of our favorite events. These cover dates from September 2016 to September 2017.*

## January

### New York Boat Show – January 25th to 29th, 2017

**Address:** Jacob K. Javits Convention Center, 655 W 34th St

**Website:** nyboatshow.com

For over 100 years people have been coming to New York City for the best in boating and fishing equipment. See hundreds of boats, yachts, canoes, and other watercraft and equipment.

Participants can also attend workshops and seminars about nautical topics given by some of the top experts in the business. Tickets are $16 for adults.

### Winter Antiques Show – January 20th to 29th, 2017

**Address:** Park Avenue Armory, 643 Park Ave

**Website:** winterantiquesshow.com

Every winter, over 70 exhibitors come to New York City to display their best antiques from Antiquity to the present.

Pieces from America, England, Europe, and Asia are represented at this fair. The entrance price is $25.

The fair can be accessed by taking the 4 or 6 to 68th St – Hunter College

### Lunar New Year Parade & Festival – January 28th, 2017

**Area:** Chinatown

**Website:** betterchinatown.com

Celebrate the Year of the Rooster in 2017 with parades of dancers, dragons, lanterns, and Chinese culture in Chinatown.

You can find the parade traveling down Mott St., under the Manhattan Bridge, and up to Forsyth St. in Lower Manhattan.

After the parade, enjoy some Chinese food or shopping in Chinatown. Get there on the Metro using the N, R, Q, 6, J, or Z train to Canal Street, or the B or D train to Grand St.

# February

## Westminster Dog Show – February 13th and 14th, 201

**Area**: Madison Square Garden, 4 Pennsylvania Plaza

Day or night you can see hundreds of different breeds of dog competing for Best in Show at the 140th Westminster Dog Show.

Events during the day take place at The Piers 92/94, (711 12th Ave at 55th Street & West Side Highway).

In the evening, they take place at Madison Square Garden, located at West 33rd Street & 7th Avenue. To get to Madison Square Garden on the subway take the 1, 2, 3, A, C, or E to 34th St/Penn Station.

# March

## New York City St. Patrick's Day Parade – March 17th, 2017

**Address**: Fifth Avenue, from 44th to 86th Streets, Manhattan

**Website**: nycstpatricksparade.org

Celebrate over 250 years of Irish culture in New York City at the St. Patrick's Day Parade. Watch as over 100,000 people march down 5th Avenue showing Irish pride with bands, bagpipes, and traditional dancing.

Afterwards, you can grab a pint at many of the Irish bars in the city. The parade starts at 11:00am at 44th St and 5th Avenue and continues to the Irish Historical Society at 79th St.

## Macy's Flower Show – 2017 dates to be determined

**Address**: Herald Square, 151 W 34th St

**Website**: www.macys.com

Head to the Macy's in Herald Square in March to see the store transformed into a garden.

Flowers from all over the world are arranged and displayed by some of the world's best. Take in all the beauty during normal business hours.

Entrance is free, but we're sure Macy's won't mind if you also make a few purchases in-store.

The quickest way to get there is to hop on the D, F, N, Q, or R train to 34th St. – Herald Square.

# April

## New York International Auto Show – April 14th to 23rd, 2017

**Address:** Jacob K. Javits Convention Center, 655 W 34th St

**Website:** www.autoshowny.com

The New York Auto Show started in 1900 and today displays over 1,000 cars and trucks, giving audiences their first glimpses at the newest cars, as well as concept designs. 2016 prices were $14 for adults & $6 for children.

Get there on the subway by taking the 7 train to 34th St/11th Ave.

## Tribeca Film Festival – April 19th to 30th, 2017

**Website:** www.tribecafilm.com

Enjoy artist talks, films, and other informative sessions about film and culture at the Tribeca Festival in Lower Manhattan. See the latest movies, many of which you cannot see anywhere else in a theater.

Enjoy talks by some of the greatest actors, directors, and cinema scholars. Prices range from $10 to $35 depending on the event.

## Cherry Blossom Festival – April 29th to 30th, 2017

**Address:** Brooklyn Botanic Garden, 990 Washington Ave

**Website:** www.bbg.org

Also called Sakuri Matsuri, the cherry blossom festival includes events and performances about Japanese culture.

You can also see the hundreds of cherry trees planted in the garden in full bloom. Prices are $25 for adults and $20 for students and seniors. There are multiple entrances to the Botanic Garden but taking the 2 or 3 train to Eastern Parkway; B, Q, or S to Prospect Park; or the 4 or 5 will get you to the garden.

# May

## NYCxDESIGN – 2017 dates to be determined

**Website:** www.nycxdesign.com

If you have an eye for good design, then come see the best of New York City in May.

Spread across the city at over 100 venues, over 200 events are organized to showcase graphic design, architecture, furniture design, urban design, fashion, and more through exhibitions, talks, trade shows, and open studios.

Most events are free to attend. Check the website for more specifics about locations.

## TD Five Boro Bike Tour – May 7th, 2017

**Website**: www.bike.nyc

If you are more of the adventurous or athletic type you can travel 40 miles across all five boroughs in one day. The tour starts in Lower Manhattan and ends with a trip on the Staten Island Ferry. You can join over 30,000 other cyclists on car-free roads all across New York City.

## Ninth Avenue International Food Festival – 2017 dates to be determined

Usually taking place in the third weekend in May, the Ninth Avenue International Food Festival offers hundreds of different styles and types of food, from savory to sweet, and from all around the world. The festival is free to the public and takes place on 9th Avenue from 42nd St to 57th St. Take an empty stomach to the 42nd St – Port Authority stop on the A, C, or E train.

# June

## Museum Mile Festival – 2017 dates to be determined

**Website**: www. museummilefestival.org

New York City has some of the best museums in the world. You can visit many of them along Museum Mile, an area along 5th Avenue from 82nd St. to 105th St. On one day in June you can visit The Metropolitan Museum of Art, The Neue Galerie, The Guggenheim, Cooper Hewitt, The Africa Center, The Jewish Museum, Museum of the City of New York, and El Museo del Barrio for free.

Enjoy car-free streets, live music, and art in the streets along with all the free museums. Get on the 4, 5 or 6 train and stop at 86th St. to enjoy all the free culture.

## River to River Festival – 2017 dates to be determined

**Website:**
www.rivertorivernyc.com

The River to River Festival takes place in Lower Manhattan and on Governor's Island. It is an arts and music festival providing access to dance, music, art, and new media. Seminars are provided that include topics about creativity and architecture. Governor's Island can be accessed by a ferry ride across the East River.

# July

## Macy's Fourth of July Fireworks – July 4th, 2017

**Website:**
www.macys.com

Celebrate the independence of America in the biggest city in the United States. The fireworks display in New York City is the largest in the country, being broadcast to viewers all over the USA. Past musical guests have included Beyoncé and Katy Perry. Macy's sets off the fireworks from 6 barges in the East River. The best places to see the fireworks are in the parks and viewing areas along the East River in Lower Manhattan and Brooklyn.

## Lincoln Center Festival – 2017 dates to be determined
**Website:** www.lincolncenterfestival.org

Lincoln Center is known for its innovative theater and dance. During the Lincoln Center Festival, the Lincoln Center arranges dance, music, theater, and puppetry performances at venues across the city.

# August

### New York International Fringe Festival – 2017 dates to be determined

**Website**: www.fringenyc.org

The Fringe Festival showcases artists from all over the world with talents in drama, opera, comedy, dance, magic, etc. With over 1,000 performances and 200 shows, there is something for every taste. The festival takes place over multiple venues spread across the West Village and East Village. Tickets are $18.

### US Open Tennis – August 28th to September 10th, 2017

**Address**: USTA Billie Jean King National Tennis Center, Flushing Meadow - Corona Park
**Website**: www.usopen.org

Travel to Queens on the 7 train to Mets – Willets Pont Station to see tennis greats battle for the final Grand Slam tournament of the year.

# September

### Electric Zoo Festival – 2017 dates to be determined

**Address**: Roosevelt Island

**Website**: www. electriczoofestival.com

The Electric Zoo Festival brings over 100,000 people from around the world to Roosevelt Island to listen and dance to some of the best electronic music and various sub-genres. If lights, dancing, and electronic beats are your idea of fun, you can get to Roosevelt Island by ferry, bus, or by walking across the footbridge. Tickets start at about $79.

### Feast of San Gennaro – September 15th to 25th, 2016

**Website**: www.sangennaro.org

Celebrate hundreds of years of Italian culture in New York City in Little Italy for 11 days. Enjoy parades, concerts, and lots of food at the annual feast.

# October

## New York Comic-Con/Anime Festival – October 6th to 9th, 2016

**Address:** Jacob K. Javits Convention Center, 655 W 34th St

**Website:** www.newyorkcomiccon.com

See all things comic, animation, fantasy, and sci-fi related at New York Comic-Con in October. See many fans in elaborate costumes as well as film screenings, booths, and panel talks by some of the world's best in the field. Take the 7 train to 34 St and 11 Ave to get there.

## Village Halloween Parade – October 31st, 2016

**Website:** www.halloween-nyc.com

In costume or not, enjoy all the wild and wacky Halloween fun in the West Village this year.

The parade progresses along 6th Avenue from Spring Street to 16th Street. It starts around 7:00pm and ends around 11:00pm. Watch as Halloween's most creative puppets, bands, and dancers march in costume. Take the A, B, C, D, E, or F train to get to 6th Avenue in the West Village.

## Open House New York Weekend – 2016 dates to be determined

**Website:** www.ohny.org

Every October, for two days, you can see the best of New York City's architecture. Visit buildings across all five boroughs, many of which are usually closed to the public.

Experience contemporary, historical, residential, and commercial architecture through visits, tours, talks, and other events celebrating the history of architecture in New York City.

# November

## TCS New York City Marathon – November 6th, 2016

**Website:** www.nycmarathon.org

Join the thousands of runners as a participant or a spectator at the New York City Marathon. Spread across the five boroughs, the race is a 26.2-mile physical feat.

## New York Comedy Festival – 2016 dates to be determined

**Website:** www.nycomedyfestival.com

New York City is a place to laugh all year round, but especially in November. Spread over 20 venues across New York City, you can see many of the world's best comedians. Last year's guests included Kathy Griffin, Margaret Cho, Ray Romano, Billy Crystal among many others. Enjoy improv shows, stand up at small or large venues, and panels discussing comedy.

## Macy's Thanksgiving Day Parade – November 24th, 2016

**Website:**
www.macys.com

Starting at 9:00am, you can be along the route of one of the most famous parades in the Unites States.

The best places to view the parade are along

6th Avenue from 38th Street to 59th Street, and along Central Park West from 59th Street to 77th Street.

Look forward to the giant balloons and the elaborate floats filled with characters, singing, and dancing. Look

out for many celebrity appearances and the beginning of Christmas season with Santa near the end of the parade.

The event is free to the public. You can also see the balloons being inflated the night before.

## Rockefeller Center Tree Lighting – November 30th, 2016

**Website:** www. rockefellercenter.com

In early December, you can be a part of Christmas magic in New

York City by attending the Rockefeller Center Tree Lighting.

Enjoy the thousands of lights be switched on at

the Rockefeller Center and get a kick start to the Christmas spirit with the famous ice skating rink and music performed by top acts.

## Radio City Christmas Spectacular – From November 11th, 2016

**Address:** Radio City Music Hall, 1260 Ave of the Americas

**Website:** www. radiocitychristmas.com

A trip to New York City would not be complete without a trip to see the world famous Rockettes

kick and dance through the Christmas season.

The show also includes dancing Santas, ballet, a Living Nativity, and of course lots of great music.

Shows begin in mid-November and end in

early January. Tickets range from about $50 to $300.

Radio City Music Hall is located near Rockefeller Center and can be easily found at the 47-50th Sts – Rockefeller Center stop on the B,D,F,M line.

## George Balanchine's The Nutcracker – Nov 25th to Dec 31st, 2016

**Address**: David H. Koch Theater, Lincoln Center, 10 Lincoln Center Plaza

**Website**: www.nycballet.com

Throughout the month of December, you can experience the best of New York ballet in the form of the world famous The Nutcracker. The ballet comprises over 200 performers, and is sure to delight people of all ages with the lights, music, costumes, and dance.

Tickets range from $75 to around $250.

The ballet takes place in the David H. Koch Theater, a part of Lincoln Center. The 1 or 2 train should get you to Lincoln Center fairly easily.

# December

## Times Square New Year's Eve – December 31st, 2016

**Website**: www.timessquarenyc.org

Brave the New York City cold with millions of other people ringing in the New Year in Times Square. Enjoy live music performed by many of the year's top artists. Watch as the famous Times Square ball drops and enjoy a kiss with a loved one to celebrate a new beginning and a new year.

# Maps

The following pages include maps of New York City's Manhattan. The map above gives you a general idea of the areas of the city which house the most attractions. These maps are not designed to be used for walking directions, but instead to give you a general sense of where different areas of the city are located in relation to each other - nevertheless major roads are included.

## MANHATTAN UPTOWN

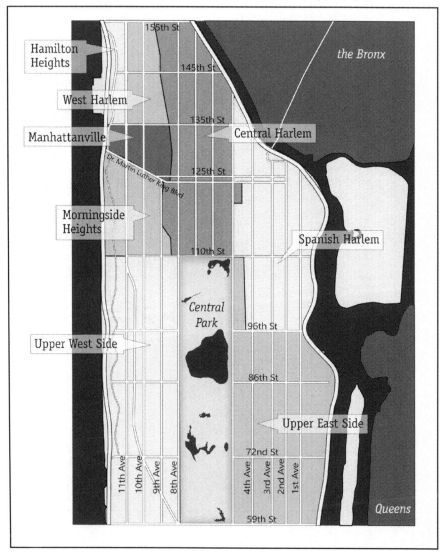

# Manhattan Midtown

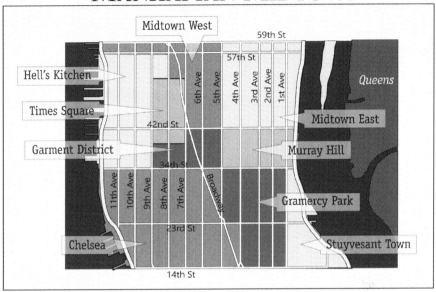

# Manhattan Downtown

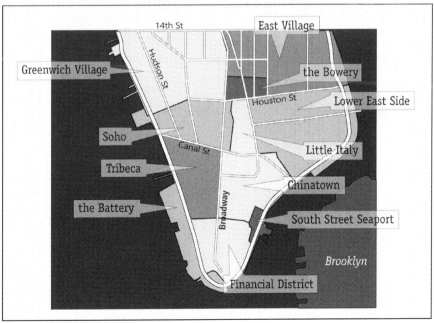

# Boroughs *of* New York City

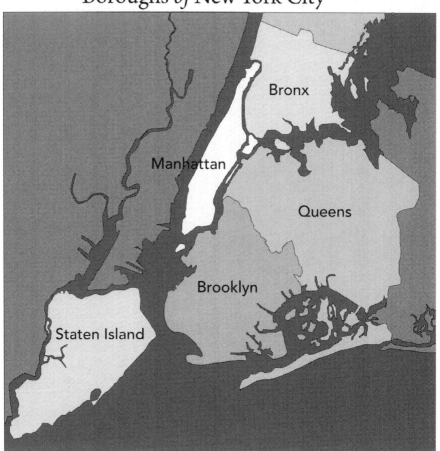

# A Special Thanks

*If you have made it this far, thank you very much for reading everything.*
*We hope this guide will make a big difference to your trip to New York City!*
*Remember to take this guide with you whilst you are visiting this amazing city.*

If you have any questions or wish to contact us, you can do so at www.
independentguidebooks.com/contact-us/. If you have any corrections, feedback
about any element of the guide, or a review of an attraction, hotel, area or
restaurant – send us a message and we will get back to you.

We also encourage you to leave a review on the Amazon website, or wherever
you have purchased this guide from. Your reviews make a huge difference in
helping other people find this guide, and we really appreciate your help.

If you have enjoyed this guide, other travel guides in this series include:

• The Independent Guide to London
• The Independent Guide to Paris
• The Independent Guide to Hong Kong
• The Independent Guide to Dubai
• The Independent Guide to Universal Orlando
• The Independent Guide to Disneyland
• The Independent Guide to Disneyland Paris
• The Independent Guide to Walt Disney World
• The Independent Guide to Universal Studios Hollywood

Have a fantastic time in New York City!

## Photo Credits:

9/11 Memorial – Edward Stojakovic; ABC No Rio – 'The All-Nite Images' (Flickr); Alice's Tea Cup – Steve Isaacs; American Folk Art Museum – Edward Blake; American Museum of Natural History – Steeven Manon; Apollo Theater – Juan Puertas; Blue Note – Satish Krishnamurthy; Brooklyn Bridge – Daniel X. O'Neil; Brooklyn Museum – Kent Wang; Bronx Zoo – Steve Harrison; Bryant Park – John Gillespie; Central Park – 'Mariko' (Flickr); Charging Bull – Sam Valadi; Chelsea Market – Mark Johnson, Coney Island – Maelick (Flickr); Cotton Club – 'Dariorug' (Flickr user); Empire State Building – Ivo Jansch; Ess-A-Bagel – Jennifer Feuchter; Five Boro Bike Tour – 'dumbonyc' (Flickr); FlatIron building – John McKerrell; Freshkills Park – Kristine Paulus; Gramercy Tavern – 'london road' (Flickr); Grand Central – Eric Wüstenhagen; Guggenheim – Vincent Desjardins; Harlem YMCA – Stefano Brivio; Hershey's – Mrs. Gemstone; Highline – David Berkowitz; Highline Hotel – Highline hotel website; Joe's Pizza – Rob Young; Katz's Delicatessen – Shelley Panzarella; La Mela – Andres Moreira; Lincoln Center – Chun-Hung Eric Cheng; Lunar New York Parade – May S. Young; Macy's – Pete Bellis; Macy's Fireworks – Joseph Bylund; Macy's Thanksgiving Day Parade – Ben W; Madison Square Park and Gramercy Park– Jeffrey Zeldman; Mamoun's and Washington Square Hotel – Alan Turkus; Metropolitan Museum of Art – Monica Arellano-Ongpin; MoMA PS1 – Jeffrey Montes; Museum of Chinese in America – Monica Wong; Museum of Sex – Maju Rezende; Mustang Thakali Kitchen – Gary Stevens; New Museum – Franklin Heijnen; New York City Fire Museum – 'State Farm' (Flickr); New York Public Library – Melanzane1013 (Flickr user); Noguchi Museum – Shinya Suzuki; Peanut Butter & Co – Uri Baruchi; Pete's Tavern, The Odeon, Brandy Library, Feast of San Gennaro and McSorley's – 'Jazz Guy' (Flickr); Prospect Park – Allison Meier; Red Rooster – Maria Eklind; Rockefeller Center – Erik Drost; Russ and Daughters – Jeffrey Bary; Serendipity 3 – Ben W; Socrates Sculpture Park – Mike Boucher; St. Patrick's Cathedral – Ben Sutherland; Stonewall Inn – 'InSapphoWeTrust' (Flickr); South Street Seaport – Ana Paula Hirama; Tenement Musuem – Tom Bastin; The Bowery Hotel – 'La Citta Vita' (Flickr); The Cornelia Street Café – Pieter Iserbyt; The Clositers – Laura Bittner; The Edgar Alan Poe Cottage – Shannon McGee; The Frick Collection – Rev Stan; The Halal Guys – Tal Atlas; The Meatball Shop – Davis Staedtler; The Standard High Line – Jessica Sheridan; The Waldorf Astoria – Chris Breeze; Times Square – Greg Knapp; Times Square New Years Eve – Anthony Quintano; Tom's Restaurant – GabboT (Flickr user); Tompkins Square Park – 'Jschauma' (Flickr); Top of the Rock – Alexandre Andre; Union Square Greenmarket – Stepan Roh; Washington Square Park – Doc Searls; and Williamsburg – Rasmus Zwickson. Cover credits: Brooklyn Bridge – Andrés Nieto Porras; Manhattan Skyline – William Warby; NYC Cab – Pascal Subtil; Statue of Liberty – Sue Waters; Times Square, Skyline small and Greenwich Village – Aurelien Guichard; Central Park – Doug Kerr; Hot dog cart – rollingrck; Tip jar – Dave Dugdale; JFK airport terminal - Eric Salard; Subway car interior - Miraage Clicks; Citibike - Omar Rawlings; Brooklyn Bridge with Skyline - Andres Nieto Porras; Times Square - Aurelien Guichard; Harlem Wall Mural - Karin; Gramercy Vintage Shop - Karen Horton; and Nuyorican Poets Cafe - Daniel X. O'Neil;

Printed in Great Britain
by Amazon